Call Adonoi

EXALTATION OF THE SUN

THE SUN, SYMBOL OF THE HEART AND WISDOM, IS RAISED BY THE LION ABOVE THE MOON. ONLY HALF OF THE MOON (UNDERSTANDING) CAN RISE ABOVE MATERIALISTIC MATTERS (I.E., THE SEA). THE PROCREATIVE ENERGIES OF THE BODY ARE REPRESENTED BY THE LION, AND THE GATES OF EXPANDED PERCEPTIONS ARE THE STARS

750

Albert L. Schutz

Call Adonoi

Manual of Practical Cabalah and Gestalt Mysticism

Quantal

Published by
QUANTAL PUBLISHING
P.O. Box 1598
Goleta, California 93017

First Edition
Printed in the United States of America 1980
Library Of Congress Catalogue No. 80-50264
ISBN 0-936596-00-7

FOR MY CO-AUTHOR, HILDA

CONTENTS

PREFACE

A book devoted to the almost forgotten rituals of dead and dying religious cults may seem out of place to the reader in an age of atomic power plants, rockets to the moon, and pocket sized computers. How could such information be of any value outside a museum devoted to ancient trivia? During the last hundred years the methods of science have been used to understand and control some of the powerful physical forces that shape our world. At the same time, a handful of men have used the same scientific methods to study the laws of the mind. Beginning with fragments of historical data, superstition, and the accidental experiences of their neighbors, the basis of mental science has been formed. Men like F.W.H. Meyers, William James, and J.B. Rhine have established the reality of extrasensory perception. Awareness of distant events, mind-to-mind communication, foreknowledge of future events, and mental influence on physical objects have been scientifically demonstrated. Though these important facts have been systematically ignored by conventional science, the work has been carried on and a growing body of information is available in such journals as the *Journal of the American Society for Psychical Research,* the *Journal of Parapsychology,* and the *Proceedings of the Parapsychology Association.*

These admittedly limited scientific studies spotlight the need to re-examine the claims and the methods of the ancient religions. Traditions that appear to be arbitrary or meaningless may hold valuable lessons for the modern student of the mind. For example, the widespread custom of repeating prayers in a forgotten language has been shown to have definite physiological influences on an individual, causing deep relaxation. It would appear that occupying the verbal centers of the mind by the prayer suppresses the constant internal chatter of the mind that keeps us busy with imagined needs and desires.

In this book, Albert Schutz introduces the results of over fifty years of investigation in Europe, the Middle East, and South America. He argues that the ancient religious art work provide the key to systematic development of the full potential of the mind. His surprising thesis is that positions of the hands shown in much religious art provide the means to properly direct the mind during meditation. Evidence for the system he describes is gathered from the religious writings of many cultures, including the oral tradition of the Bektashi Sufis. However, the proof of his argument was established by experiments. This book provides the basic information for such experiments.

How could the hands play such an important role in meditation? Of course the first objective of meditation is to control the mind, and concentration, regardless of the object, provides exercise in control. Perhaps the posture of prayer can provide a psychic linkage with mystics of the past. In clairvoyance experiments, a name, photograph, or a piece of clothing have been used as a psychic address to locate other information about a certain person. Thus the ritual posture of meditation may serve to locate the thoughts of the ancient mystics. Some ancient traditions describe a non-physical field that surrounds the body and regulates its growth and function. Possibly the position of the hands could influence the function of such a field.

By presenting a well organized summary of the ancient tradition *Call Adonoi* offers each of us the chance to discover for ourselves what these rituals can do.

Dr. David Phillips
UCSB

November 11, 1976

ACKNOWLEDGEMENTS

Rabbi ISRAEL B. KOLLER
Dr. DAVID PHILLIPS U.C.S.B.
ED TAFOYA
MARGARET WILLIAM
OSCAR LOWENSCHUSS Sc.D.
ANNE N. LOWENKOPF, Editor
LEE & SHERMAN STARR

I sincerely thank them for their encouragement and help they so freely gave.

CREDIT FOR THE ILLUSTRATIONS

Designs by DAN GHENO
KNIGHTS TEMPLAR, Ezra A. Cook
Reproductions from the authors collection.

Book Design by Jim Cook/Atypical Typesetting

There is nothing amiss in this book. Nevertheless
Should you find inadequacies, complete them;
Should you find errors, correct them;
Should you meet with mutilation in the language,
Or in the letters — more or less — improve them.
And do not scorn the work, for man's
Beset with forgetfulness and carelessness...
The Secret of the Gnostics

Hamza Fan Suri

INTRODUCTION

When six hundred-thousand Israelites on Mount Sinai received God's law, each one of them understood it differently; for this reason, so the Rabbis said, the Bible can be interpreted in sixty myriad ways.

For the author, the Bible is not only a historical narrative, a guide to spiritual, moral, rational truth, wisdom and a Law given verbatim by God, but also the body of man.

This is one of the hidden aspects of the Bible, emblematically shown by the free-masons when they let the neophite place his hands in various postures on the holy book. The profound reason for this act is no longer understood in the modern fraternity. The laying on of hands in prescribed ways is the work of the *oral Bible*, known as the Cabalah of God; and this is the content of my book.

MASONIC CEREMONY IN THE YEAR 1875

GIANT GATE, ST. STEPHEN CHURCH (VIENNA)

PROLOGUE

Standing in front of the St. Stephen Cathedral in Vienna, our teacher, August Hoffmann, pointed with a sweeping gesture to the main portal and explained: "The two big pillars on the sides of the portal are emblematic for Jakhin and Boas, the pillars on King Solomon's Temple. I want you to examine them now very carefully. See if you can find a symbol that should not be on a church."

We gazed with little enthusiasm, being sure that our answer would be wrong. Waiting only a few moments he waved again in the general direction of the weatherbeaten front and continued: "You should have noticed first of all that the pillars are not exactly below the center of the windows. Now, this is meaningful! And the capitals have as ornaments a phallic symbol on the right and a vulva on the left side of the portal. Well? Why should these symbols be on a Gothic church?"

After this question, he gave a lecture right there on the Plaza about the fascinating history of the guilds of the Free-masons. They were not only builders, he said, but custodians of secret traditions. They hid their "heretic" heritage in the decorations, statues, and ground-plans of the churches. And the Catholic clergy did not realize that these churches were monumental textbooks of the Jewish Cabalah, a fact not known even today.

"...and just as in medieval times," concluded the teacher, "the ancient esoteric lores are not lost today. The so-called hidden sciences are all around us, free for all who want to know them; they cannot be forgotten either, since they are a part of our being."

Even so, I did not find it easy to discover ancient esoteric doctrines. They are scattered in thousands of coded books, on works of arts, ornaments and architectural designs. They are integral parts of the fundamental teachings of religions and so much a part of our life that we hardly notice them, just as we are rarely aware of breathing constantly.

In this book the occult that is a part of everybody's life and yet recondite will be probed with the help of an old esoteric handbook.

INTRODUCTION TO THE PRACTICAL CABALAH

1. The Esoteric Teachings of Today

The interest in mysticism in all its varieties has rapidly increased in recent years. One reason is of course curiosity. Another, the realization that the religious establishments, sciences, and philosophy fail to solve the personal problems of the daily life. But the main reason is the realization that the increased mastering of the external life, has not produced a corresponding development and understanding of our inner nature. As always in times of great stress, people are turning more and more to mysticism. They appear like a spiritual catch-as-catch-can, passing from abracadabra to Zen, for some escape routes from reality, for others a search for inner peace.

When studying some of the newer cults, we become aware that they do not teach something really new. The ideas they promote, the experiences they have and are ready to give to others for a price, the paths they proclaim to be the only right ones, are ancient teachings using updated terminology. Eventually, the search for a greater understanding of the self leads back to the great sources of wisdom that have been with us at all times.

For serious students the important field of the occult is not treated with the attention it deserves; there is very little known today about the integrated esoteric teachings of ancient academies.

The study and understanding of ancient teachings is indispensable to the development of workable modern approaches to religions and cults.

Our text is the little known training manual that was written for use of initiation cults and schools of priests, kings and prophets in ancient times. However, its coded language, archaic symbols, and references do not reveal the basic esoteric teaching we seek. As reference-book it did not reveal the real secrets which the initiates had received by word-of-mouth. The real problem is to find this oral tradition.

My book is based upon "The Book of Formation" (Sefer Jezirah) whose age is highly controversial.

2. Codes of the Cabalah

The Cabalah is the sum of all the esoteric teachings in Judaism. We speak of a practical and a theoretical Cabalah. The name Cabalah is generally translated as "tradition" and should be understood as "oral tradition".

Among the existing two thousand books and manuscripts relating to the Cabalah, not one presents the practical Cabalah in ways that could be understood by the uninitiated. Allusions are hidden in codes that few scholars can translate. There are over one hundred codes used in one system alone, known as the Temurah in which letters are changed by means of anagrams.

Another complex code-system is the Gematria, in which letters are turned into numbers (the origin of numerology). The sum of these numbers are then used as keys for other words.

In addition to the coded shorthand of the notaricon in which a letter can represent a word, an idea, or whole sentences, each Hebrew letter has also a cabalistic meaning.

Another system known primiarly from the Psalms of David, are the acrostics. Here the letters are placed in specific ways to give the initiate relevant information.

For the cabalist, the most important codes are specific numbers that alert the student to the underlying meaning of the paragraphs. For instance, the number three is mentioned as the "Three Mothers," seven is the "seven doubles" etc.

These codes fired the imagination of medieval cabalists whose works are loaded with new codes. Their most common system was to read words backwards. This childish approach was used in every conceivable language. The Torah became Tarot, kakos, sokak, kallas, and sallak. This device and many others, some more complicated made the literature of the medieval periods boring reading and unpalatable.

However, when the serious student works with these codes, each word leaps across space and time, to loose its surface meaning. The mind grows acustomed identifying stories of God, the universe, angels, demons, the physical world and its history, as symbols for a hidden reality. And eventually the intellect is challenged to find what this reality is.

3. Sources of the Study

The cabalistic teachings had never been systematically recorded in ancient times. The references in the Scriptures and commentaries to their practical aspects present considerable difficulties, even for the initiated. Places of learning existed in Israel at all times; schools educated the patriarchs and their sons, the priests and kings in the secret lores, even during the Exodus. Besides the academies of Shem, Heber, Hillel, and Shamai, other schools existed in Jerusalem, in Israel, and after the destruction of the Second Temple, in Babylon. Most of the oral teachings were eventually forgotten by the Jews during the many persecutions they suffered during the following 2000 years. However, the oral teachings were not lost.

The author attempted to uncover the basic cabalistic teachings by searching for initiates in Jerusalem. However, supposedly well-versed cabalists refused to discuss or even admit any knowledge of the subject. The reasons for not discussing the Cabalah were many: "The less one talks about these matters, the better". "I will loose the benefit of all my labor". "It is dangerous to enter the field without due preparations". All of these comments are true, not only of the occult, but for working on high-voltage power lines, taming a lion, or driving a car.

After futile attempts to piece decoded hints from several cabalistic books into a coherent picture, the only recourse was to find remnants of the basic practical teachings in places outside of Israel, where Jews had lived comparatively peaceful lives for long periods and would be less constrained. The author hoped that the oral tradition of the cabalists had not disappeared completely in such countries and that non-Jews had been initiated into Jewish occult doctrines. Luckily this had been the case.

The most likely countries were Arabia and Yemen, in which the Jews had occasionally been rulers before the rise of Islam. Jewish literature especially the Bible, legends, traditions, and, what is of greatest interest for us, Jewish occult teaching, became part of the foundation of the Islamic faith.

In the traditional tales of early Islamic history we find that the prophet's occult knowledge came from a Jewish sage Ben-Ghazi. As two Jewish tribes helped Mohammad to gain power, "The priestly tribes" Banu Nadir and Banu Qurayza (Koresh). Mohammad from the clan of Hashim (Ha-Shem) was a member of the tribe of the Banu Qurayza and in consequence Jewish. Historically unreliable as these tales are, the early occult tradition of Islam shows similarity to the Jewish occult. For this reason alone the teaching of the Sufis (Islamic Mystics, Dervishes, Fakirs) are of interest for our study.

Other comparatively quiet places were Georgia, the Crimean Peninsula and the Don Delta (all in Russia now), where parts of the tribe of Dan (Danann, Danao) supposedly had lived for a long time in peaceful coexistence with a polyglot population. The stories about these little known Jewish kingdoms sound fantastic, but this is what tradition tells us.

When the area was invaded by Norseman and Celts, a part of the tribe fled to the Caucasus. We find that Hebrew words, number systems, and exercises formed a part of the magical Caucasian Yoga. The "strong men" of the tribe of *Dan* (Dan-Ḥassaks) remained in the neighborhood of the river *Don*. Other segments of the tribe moved with the Cimmerians and Celts up the river *Dan*ube through Europe, came to *Dan*mark, and settled eventually in Ireland. Some ancient legends of Ireland and Wales definitely come from the Middle East. When Christian missionaries landed in Ireland, they found to their surprise that Celtic heathens had Biblical names.

Whether the magic use of the runic alphabet was developed with the help of the Jews from the Rhineland, who settled there before the Nordic tribes had come to the west, or through the influence of the tribe of Dan is difficult to determine. However the Hebrew alphabet was used by the Norsemen very much as the I-Ching was employed in China—as a tool of prophecy and guidance.

According to the epic poem, the Edda, All-Father Odin brought the magic of the Runes to the Norsemen from the Middle East, the center of three continents. Quite a number of these Nordic Gods had names coming from the Middle Eastern area. Among them is Odin (Adon) and his son Baalder (Baal-Or), the shiny god who dies "on the tree"; Loki (Logos), the god of fire, and the god who gave life to the Nordic race, Haimdal (Ḥaim=life in Hebrew). The word Dan is in several names of Gods, such as *Don*-Ar, Wo-*Dan*, *Dan*-Aor etc. The world tree on which Wodan sacrificed himself for *three* days and gave one eye as the price for wisdom, the serpent on the foot of the tree, and the rivers coming from the roots, are from the Garden of Eden story.

These are some of the clues that led the author to look in the Islamic and Nordic mystic traditions for the secrets of the practical Cabalah.

4. Sufism and the Islamic Oral Tradition

Islamic mysticism comes from cabalistic lore. At the time of the Prophet's death, forty different occult sects, known as Darvishes existed. The number forty could have been a code number. The code will be explained later. The Prophet Mohammed received fourteen words of power for contemplation at the end of his initiation. Later, these words were attached to the opening phrases of specific chapters of the Koran by the compiler, the second Caliph Abu Bakr. These fourteen words are also ciphers like the seven doubles in the Book of Formation, the fourteen years bondage of Jacob for Rachel and Lea, the fourteen Stations, of the Cross, and fourteen severed parts of the body of Osiris.

The history of the early Islamic mystics, the Sufi orders, make fascinating reading. The darvish teachers incorporated the complete ceremonies and exercises of Jewish mysticism into their teachings. We have benefited greatly from the frankness with which the Sufi teachers discussed these occult matters.

We find in their literature over and again evidence that their ideas about God, the universe, the world and the corresponding systems and laws of human development derived from ancient Jewish tradition, especially from the cabalistic Book of Formation. This is especially noticable in the writings of the Persian mystic Fazl-Ullah (ca. 1397), the founder of the darvish sects of the Hurufis. His teachings became part of the dogma of the sect of the Bektashis in Turkey.

At the beginning of this century a German seaman, Rudolf Glauer, who changed his name later to Count Heinrich von Sebottendorf, acquired from the Turkish Bektashis' rites, one of the most jealously kept secrets of the Sufis, the Ulm el Miftaḥ (Science of the Key).

In 1808 approximately 53,000 Bektashis were put to death or sent into exile by Mahmut II in Turkey. The Turkish Republic, as well as the Albanian government, surpressed the sect again in 1925-1946. As a result, the once powerful holy council of the Bektashis ceased to exist. The last monastery at the foot of Mokattam Hill in Cairo was closed in 1957 by Abd el Nasser. Whatever the writer knows about the secrets of the Bektashi, learned from the last five members that lived in this beautiful monastery, now a museum. These exercises in mysticism are identical to those of the Italian freemasons and the practical Cabalah.

5. Medieval Cults

The relationship between the Moslims, Christians, and Jews during the middle ages had never been good. However when they were at peace with each other, the diverse Sufi sects welcomed European students. Crusaders were initiated at such times, spreading the occult knowledge they had received on their way home. As a result we find Hebrew words and cabalistic exercises frequently quoted and used in books, cults, or secret societies all over Europe. This knowledge was the core of the cults of the Middle ages, such as the famous Templars, Knights of the Grail, Rosicrucians, Freemasons, and Illuminaties.

During the same period, Jewish scholars and philosophers in Germany, Italy and Spain, rediscovered their cabalistic heritage. Great cabalistic schools sprang up in the south of France, Sicily and Palestine. Much later, as soon as the Turkish invaders were driven out, a cabalistic-minded movement developed in Galicia, Poland. This movement is known today as the Chassidim. Unfortunately their cabalistic knowledge is at best perfunctory; cabalistic teachings are no longer a part of organized Jewish religion.

Europe at this time was dominated by the Roman Catholic clergy and the occult was declared heresy. Crusaders who returned to Europe as initiates of Sufism dared not divulge their knowledge. Those who were bold enough to speak out, usually had to pay with their lives.

To avoid persecution, the new mystics used allegories to spread their knowledge. Fables (Grail, Arthurian legends) masqued with the sometimes weird terminologies of the sciences and trades of their time, became the hiding place of their rituals. This is the reason behind the development of the magical card-games Tarot and many of the odd tales, terms, and pictures of alchemy and astrology.

But the most ingenious group to circumvent the inquisition of the church were the builders of churches, the Freemasons. These organizations of master-builders could move freely from one town to another at a time when all other tradesmen were bound to the churches, nobility, knights, and kings. Not so confined, the Free-masons spread the esoteric knowledge of the Cabalah disguising their secrets in the terms of the building trade and teaching them in different initiation-rites that centered around Salomonic legends. The Freemasons taught in carefully calibrated degrees of mysticism, beginning with the first stage after many years of trial. The apprentice eventually became a "Master Mason".

To record a text of their knowledge the secrets of the Cabalah were put into the designs of gothic ground plans, transposing words into symbols. For example, to show the importance of the right arm in Cabalah, the cruceiform floor-plan had a chapel on the right side of the cross, at an angle of 45 degrees. The arrangement explained away to church officials as marking the angle of Christ's head on the Cross. All the gesture, stances and numerical arrangements of Gothic statues contain cabalistic information. Church windows became the mandalas of Christianity.

When the building-guilds gradually became open trades, most of the teachings sunk into oblivion. A group of intellectuals in London rediscovered the occult in the early 1700s and organized the "Speculative Masons" that became todays "Free and Accepted Masons".

The real secrets of the Cabalah are by now almost completely forgotten in their rituals. Only the symbols, systems, and outer forms of the cermonies are still left. The older books on Freemasonry, however, show that the deeper teachings were known and understood at the time of the rediscovery in the 1700s.

6. Religious Art as Source Material

Early religious works of art are a valuable source for the study of occult lore. They not only reveal what the scriptures concealed but point to some strange fields of knowledge that are little known in modern times. One is the "holding of the hands."

Rather strange gestures of the hands are found on megalithic statues, cave-paintings and monumental petroglyphs. Identical gestures were used on works of art in historic times, but their meaning only partially revealed in religious scriptures. They are of utmost importance for our study of ancient occult concepts. Universal in scope, these gestures show how the "secret work of the right hand" was executed.

The emphasis on numbers, gestures and stances of the esoteric teachings, found on religious artworks all over the world is an ancient form of preserving and transmitting knowledge. The gestures and ornaments regarded by most people as "artistic inspiration" are in reality guides and symbols of innermost secret of *all* religions. The artworks used the designs of gods, nature spirits, life and death of culture heroes, the creation and destruction of the Universe to illustrate the working-methods, laws, powers, and nature of the self. Many occult emblems are still used conventionally by modern artists in the Orient and in India, but in western civilizations occult evidences were destroyed or lost.

During the author's work as a restorer of church paintings, he became familiar with the strict regulations concerning the decorating of Byzantine churches.

Contrary to common belief, these religious works are not mere decorative designs or traditional Christian symbols, but guides to the occult tradition of the early Christian Orthodox Church. The coding of Byzantine artwork was regulated by textbooks for church painters, such as the "Codex Byzantinicum" and "Dionysios the Painter." The Roman Catholic Church became suspicious of Byzantine symbolism and destroyed it in an art-war known as the Iconoclasm (718-816). Christian mysticism went underground.

The comparison of hand gestures, colors, stances and symbolic animals on the pictures of Christ, saints, and religious figures before and after the Iconoclasm, give some interesting clues to practical aspects of early Christian mysticism.

The most important clues to the deciphering of the hieroglyphics of designs are: 1) *the holding of the hands* and the stances of the feet (footsteps) as symbols of the three paths of enlightment; 2) the *numbers* and designs of implements held and the selection of right or left hand to do the holding, the numbers of ornaments, marks on the body, and the number of attendants, judges, consorts, and followers, whether human, animals or merely ornamental design; and 3) the *colors* of fields, figures and the changes of hues on identical forms. So an identical figure may be painted completely red, blue, black or white in orderly sequence. These colors, stances of the body, signs of the hands and numbers indicate the attained level on the way to perfection.

Here is one example of the way the artwork relates to the mystical disciplines. In the early stages of study, during the work of the purification, the neophyte will quite unexpected, be faced by his true self. This momentous moment, when the self is met "face to face" does not only come during meditations; J.W. von Goethe met his "other" self during a walk in the park. *Excerpts from notes of students and the author:*

> New York, Aug. 2, 1962. Read about a gnostic deity Yaldabaoth; use the name as word of power in a meditation. Hold the hands in pyramid-sign over the heart, repeating "Yaldabaoth." See almost at once in wide-angle view a tremendous sandy plain covered with *sulphur-colored* foam. On heavy *black* cumuli clouds an invisibly setting sun outlines a gigantic face of a *lion* in dirty orange colors. The apparition has the breast of a woman, claws of a beast. The tail that thrashes the ground ends in a serpent-head; a *black* cloud had turned into a *lion*. The apparition stares emotionless ahead not focused on anything, but danger radiates from this figure as if ready to jump. Great discomfort, stopped meditation.

According to text-books yalda-ba-oth looked very much like the author's vision. The aramaic name means: girl-coming-as-sign. "Girl" is one of the terms for the soul-forces, others are: virgin, bride, mother, queen etc.

The author was not aware that he had seen the guardian of the treshold.

Goleta, Oct. 22, 1971
J. would like to meet the guardian of his spiritual world. He knows that in this experience he will see his own soul in its present state of imperfection.

A sad looking J. told me next morning somewhat reluctant what had happened in his meditation. He used the sign of the pyramid on his breast with the word of power "ELOHIM" instead of "ADONOI".

"I saw something — but this cannot be my soul? I was in a room, the walls covered with *black* courtains. I laid on the floor on a *yellow-golden* rug, curled up as a dog!!!" he laughed "this cannot be my soul..."

When you see your soul for the first time, your eyes open up. You are ashamed as Adam and Eve in the paradise when they saw themselves. The author shrank away from such a confrontation. Castaneda in his "Separate Reality" met his guardian and could not prevail. He took the position known from the caucasian yoga as Guatama

LION STANCE: CAUCASIAN YOGA

Buddhas' *lion* stance. While reclining on his right side his left hand pressed on the ground with the arm in a square. Castaneda found himself in a *pale-yellow* gaseous looking landscape attacked by a *black* gnat. Before closing in, the insect veered off.

Mrs. L. S. Barbara Aug. 28, 1974: Was lying in bed doing "MIH" handposition, eyes open. Saw a swarm of *black* flies come at me, then recede in a pulsating motion.

Many details in these experiences, the smell and color of burning sulphur, the black color, the archtypal winged figures like lions, herald the confrontation with the occult "self". Imperfect itself, it will block the treshold to higher knowledge for all that are not yet prepared. This will be explained in another chapter.

Occult literature is filled with the descriptions of encounters with guardians that will not let you advance unless able to answer "their three questions" and know how to ask them in turn. These are the sphinxes, Cerberus, devourer of the heart, Yaldabaoth, etc.

Although the meeting of the guardian is a different experience for each person, the emblems for this meeting are identical. They give in stenoform the essential clues to the mechanics that led to the experiences: the hands with claws, the tail ending in a serpent head, a tongue sticking out, usually but not necessarily, from a feline head.

All over the world and in all ages, the signs of blessing were identical, except that the

BALINESE MUDRA

LEVITICAL BLESSING

hands and the *fingers* moved differently during the blessing in the various faiths. About the reasons for these movements of hands and fingers very little is known today.

MASONIC SIGN

Movements of the body, especially those of the hands and fingers, during the services of temple dances is a kinetic record of this knowledge. The fascinating gestures and dancing of the Tibetan monks can still be studied *in vivo,* but if we wait long enough, we will loose this source of information too. One of the gestures during the Tibetan prayers is a movement in which the right hand is held over the left and then reversed. This gesture is found not only on Tibetan works of art, but on statues and stealas of Indian gods, especially of Kali and in the few Mayan codexes that were not burned. The Freemasons call this gesture a sign of obligation, and the cabalists make identical gestures during their preparative exercises *on the body.*

A comparison of ancient art shows that none of the basic occult concepts were the property of one religious faith only or of one privileged group of mystics.

GESTALT-MYSTICISM

Gestalt theories examine the totality of a structure. Each part of a "Gestalt" requires certain conditions and a fixed place to function properly within the whole. What happens to each part of this structure is determined by an intrinsic law inherent within the whole. A comprehension of this law is the aim of Gestalt-mysticism.

Gestalt-mysticism considers the corpus of a religion and its occult lores as a whole in which the descriptions of the mystical experiences are a key to the understanding of its working. Comparative studies of unrestricted descriptions of mystical experiences are the sources for the psychology of expanded perception, but the laws pertaining to this branch of psychology are essentially the laws of the Gestalt and holistic theories.

Mystical experiences come from the unconscious, from energies that are the cause of all benevolent and destructive changes in the microcosmos of man. To understand and, eventually, to master the inner vital energies, the student of the occult learns by expanding his perceptions.

A problem in the study of mystical experiences is that one and the same perception cannot be experienced again, since to do so the perceiving person would have to have one and the same attitude, clarity of mind and power of concentration. Yet there are more recondite reasons that such experiences cannot be duplicated. They will be explained in another part of the book.

To make a study of experiences feasible, and this is necessary since they are a key to the "Law," we look for certain recurring phenomena within the state of altered consciousness. These experiences come in a variety of symbols, moods or bodily signals and *they* are the criterion of the genuineness of a vision.

They appear through exercises performed under controlled conditions where one part of the body interacts with other parts. The exercises create stimuli from the sense of touching and kinesthesia of the stances, grips, signs, movements, and complex asanas of various creeds. Other stimuli come from sight, sounds, smells and other sense experiences. Combined they comprise a field of controllable stimuli: controllable, because they are not haphazardly applied but follow strict rules of application in time and space.

To show how the mystical Gestalt theory is applied to the framework of a faith, here is one of the least known systems of controllable psychological stimuli: "The psychic exercises of the Cabalah." Other exercises include the relationship of the psychic to the classical religious tradition, the conceptual and the magical practices of archaic Judaic tradition.

THE SPIRITUAL EXERCISES

This manual is designed both for beginning mystics who want a program of exercises to advance their spiritual awareness and students of comparative religion who can use the descriptions of the signs and their variations to trace the practice of essentially the same mystical exercises around the world.

That oral tradition, called Torah, Cabalah, or simply "the Law" teaches the student how to observe the commandments of God. The ancient sages said that we follow the commandments best by doing "pious deeds". The phrase "pious deeds" means that we follow the commandments even when their significance is not understood.

The practical Cabalah is a part of these commandments. When the author was confronted with the system of its secret exercises, the reason they were not revealed became obvious. Although the results of pious deeds are desirable, the methods seem strange, even absurd.

In the first exercises seemingly meaningless gestures are made with the hands and strange words repeated at the same time. After about one week of such meditations, heat-sensations and vibrations emanate from the fingertips and palms. The energies that emerge from the hand are in equally strange ways led to the body by the "laying on the hands." With these practices you will find your awareness expands in most remarkable ways and you will perceive sensory signals on the body that you had not noticed before. When the signals are understood and followed, you will be in posession of a key to the understanding of the self.

This is the start of exercises that lead to the "royal road" or "way to perfection"; inculcated in four stages. Terms for this work are: awakening, activating, purification, perfection or child, student, fighter and wise man. The Freemasons call them entered apprentice, journey-man, master-mason and master-of-the-lodge.

The exercises themselves are "the work of the hand" paraphrased in the Bible as "the right hand of God, His breath and Word that created the world".

Three hidden subjects have to be considered; the work of the hand, specific ways of breathing and the use of "lost" words.

On the next level various parts of the body begin to oscillate. These are the first signs of awakening the "points or gates of higher perceptions". During the activating and later in the purification exercises, abilities emerge from these points that are known nowadays as E.S.P., *E*xpanded *S*ensory *P*erception. Accelerated by the powers of the enlivened hands the activating brings harmonious feelings of health, well being and strength to body and mind.

During the following work of purification energies known as the serpent of the paradise, or serpent-fire well up in the body to dissolve negative concepts that block the way to perfection.

On the forth level reality is perceived "from afar." The old concepts "die" and are replaced by a new understanding of the self and the world. Once the energies of the fiery serpent are subdued, the student gains access to the road to higher knowledge.

Only an orderly sequence of 1. exercises, 2. studies, and 3. prayers guaranty *safe* access to tremendous powers that are dormant in the unconscious.

Many questions crop up during exercises: How often and in what sequence should each exercise be performed? Is there an optimum time of day, month, full or new moon? Do I need to take a bath, wear ceremonial cloth or go naked? Should I have periods of fasting and keep dietary law?

The answer: Do what you *feel* is right to do and act in accordance with religious teachings.

During the studies and meditations "the law" is revealed and from this moment on you will *know* the correct order of your contemplations and exercises.

7. Code Number Three

AWAKENING

The exercises of the hands have the names of the ancient elements of fire, water and air. The signs made by the hands and the words of power are contemplated during the exercises. They were universally known in somewhat modified form by the various world religions and cults. For comparative studies and experiments some of these variations and words are included in this chapter.

The awakening exercises are made with the right hand by men and the left hand by women.

a. SIGN OF FIRE

The index finger is held straight. The other fingers form a fist or a circle with the thumb. Fingertips do not touch. Word: "mih" (MEEH)

Glyphs: 

Variations:

Index and small finger point up, the other form a circle with the thumb. This sign is found on Christian, Indian, Tibetan and Chinese works of art.

Index and middle finger bunched, the other fingers form a cross with the thumb—another Christian variation.

Thumb and index finger form a cross, the others point up or lay flat on the palm. Greek Orthodox Church, Mayan and modern Latin Americans all have artwork that

indicates their use of this form of the exercise.
Alternate words of power: (I pronounced EEEE) HIM, CHRI-STI, SI-RI, IS-IS. LI-LITH.

BASIC SIGN OF FIRE

UNIVERSAL SIGN OF FIRE

CHRISTIAN VERSION OF THE SIGN OF FIRE

b. SIGN OF AIR

Fingers are spread apart, held straight or curved to resemble an open claw.
Word: "mah" (a as in apple)
Glyphs: L ⊥
Variations:

Middle and ring finger bunched.
Little, ring, middle and index finger bunched (lion-grip)

Alternate words of power: amen, alam, ra,na,ab-ram.

SIGN OF AIR (TIBETAN)

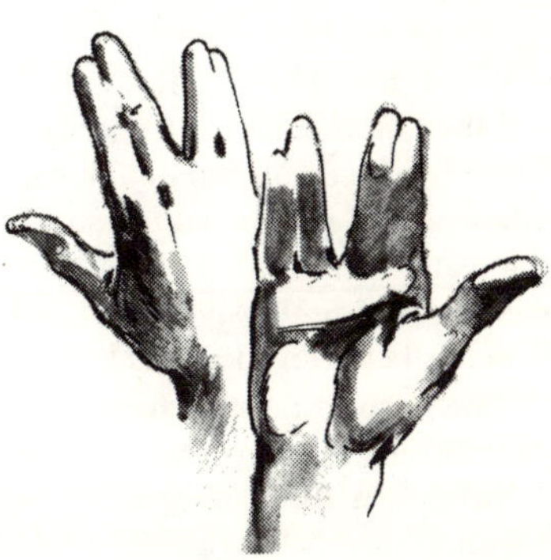

SIGN OF BLESSING AND HEALING

c. SIGN OF WATER

Index finger and thumb form a circle. Fingertips do not touch. Word: "hou" The ou is pronounced as written, a cross between o & u.
Glyphs: O G
Variations:
Thumb and middle finger form a circle called sign of intelligence.
Thumb and ring finger form a circle called sign of health.
Thumb and little finger form a circle called source of psychic power.
Thumb and all fingers form a circle called the sign of wisdom.
Alternate words of power: ZOTH, MOU, OUM, ON, GOU-ROU.

SIGN OF "OUM"

INDIAN VARIATION

d. HOLDING THE POWER

A fist with the thumb held in or outside is the hand of power. Evidence of this exercise is found on Egyptian, Mesopotamian and Tibetan works of art.

HAND OF POWER

Each sign relates to a specific vibration alluded to "as the word of power" that we repeat during the exercises. This word, is spoken in the "great voice," meaning that it is spoken without the sound being heard. The vibrations of the word emanate in the throat and are projected mentally in turn to the hand, the spine and eventually to the whole body.

When the vibrations reach their peak strength, peculiar heat-sensations emanate from fingertips and palm. These vibrations become distinctly different for each of the signs of the hand. The vibrations of the fire sign shoot up in (or along side) the finger. In the water meditations rings of air seem to rise for the hand. When contemplating the sign of air, you will feel waves of warm, dry air flowing between the thumb and the index finger, often swinging like a pendulum.

The signs of the hands on works of art are often concealed by implements, decorations, background ornaments, and glyphs. These features provide additional information for iconographic studies. The number of arms, legs, heads and their various colors, decorations, and symbols may indicate the diverse levels of initiation depicted or the sequential series of stances and the correct movements during meditative dancing. The various implements held in the hands of "Gods" are clues to the words of power used in each of the stances.

The implements for the sign of fire are generally linear. They consist of pillars,

FLAMING SWORD AND SIGN OF FIRE

sceptres, swords, maces, staffs, crosses, or tridents. The glyphic stenoforms—parts that stand for the whole—are three prongs, leashes, fingers, thunderbolts, or plain straight lines. A great variety of serpent- and dragon-symbols stands for the fire in its active state, winding around trees, roots, on staffs, heads, seats, flying, walking or fighting man.

The implements for the sign of water, as well as its stenoforms, are round. They are represented by globes, apples, diadems, cauldrons, cups, or bells held by gods or kings, or items decorated with circles, fishes, water drops. The finest symbol for water is the yin-yang that contains five correlated glyphs for water and materia.

DIONYSOS AND SEMELE

TIBETAN

Emblems for the air are usually square. They are either blocks, books, pyramids, buildings or builder-squares. Their decorations display wings, birds, feathers, clouds, veils, or a heart resting on the palm of the hand, blessed or held up to the sun.

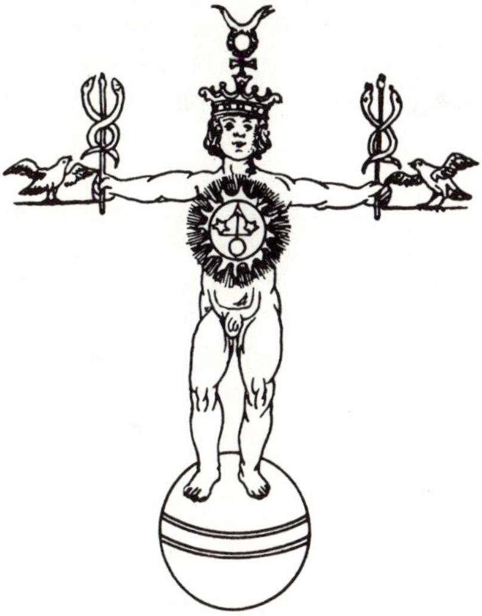
MERCURY IN ALCHEMY

The mediaeval alchemists choose Greek gods and their emblems as symbols for the elements. Their confusing designs usually show god Vulcan as fire; god Mercury and his winged symbols for air; Greek godesses with moon sickles on head, dress or under the feet were emblematic for water, salt, and materia prima.

The alchemists called the three elements sulphur, salt, and mercury that had to be compounded in the crucible to transform lead to gold. "In the crucible of the leaden body ignorance was transformed to wisdom." As a signal for the start of the mainworks: "the great chymical operation", the index finger emitted sulphurous fumes. This was followed by the taste of mercury sublimate on the same spot and eventually by a saline taste between thumb and index finger that marked the end of the preparation.

In the mediaeval mystery-plays, the secret of the three elements was revealed by presenting three culprits that by initials, names or symbols could be identified as elements, as for instance JUBEL-A, JUBEL-O and JUBEL-UM. Being first malefactors, they became benefactors at the end of the performance when with their help the slain culture-hero was resurrected.

The words of powers are attributes of the creator. Used during meditations the vibrations of the word form new life-patterns in the subtle body that are difficult to erase. Because of the danger inherent in this knowledge and the hidden effects that the words have on mind and body, they were not revealed.

In the ancient academies religious leaders and priest-kings learned how to manipulate these words of power. As initiates they aquired the ability with the help of words and phrases to imprint faith and trust in their subjects. But more important still, by knowing the names of energies and entities, the initiates could fearlessly approach and utilize formation powers.

The most universal of all the words of power is "AMEN". The sages claimed that "a

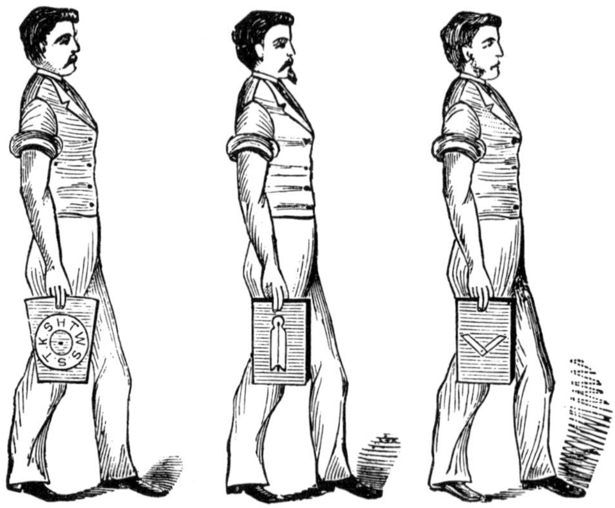

MASONIC MARKSMEN

prayer without amen has no power", or "amen is the working-tool of God." The Church, fully aware of occult potency of the word amen, included it in the mass. It was not just a phrase to conclude prayers, but an integral part of the worship, later known as the "great amen." The word is repeated for extended periods by the choir and the congregation, just like the "Oum" and "Mou" in the eastern religions.

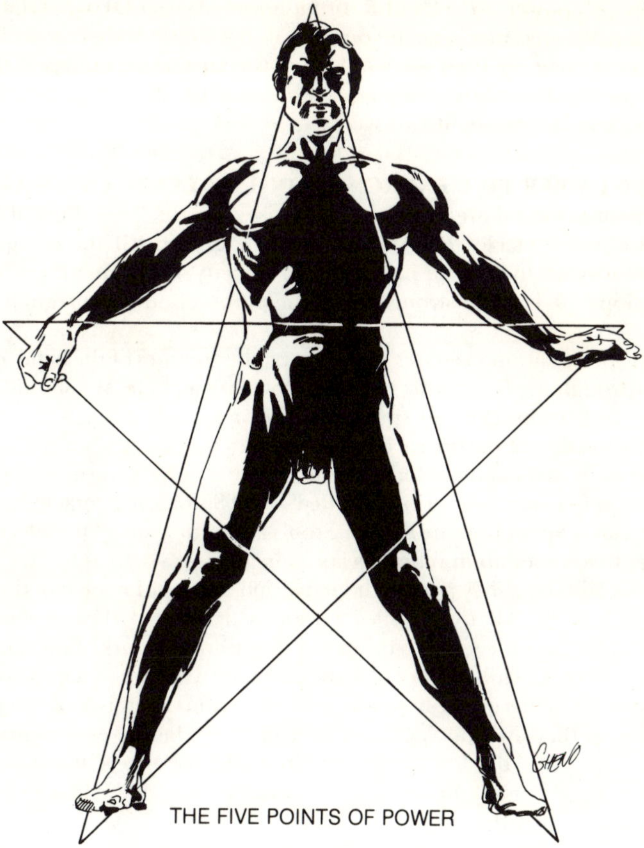

THE FIVE POINTS OF POWER

8. Code Number Five
The Sources of Hidden Energies

THE SOURCES OF HIDDEN ENERGIES

Although only one hand is activated at first, other parts of the body respond unexpectedly during the meditations. The second hand may become, as if by accident, sensitized at the beginning of the exercises. In fact, the vibrations of the hand not concentrated upon, may occasionally be extremely strong. These common experiences will happen again at the activating of the seven gates of higher perception and eventually even in the "visions of the night."

The vibratory signals come from the unconsciousness to show us the areas of the body that should be activated or call our attention to exercises not well done.

a. PRAXIS

In all stances of the exercise number five we stand with the legs apart, holding the arms almost horizontal. "Never to lift the arms above the head unless in prayers." While the stance remains the same in all exercises, the energies that now emanate from the hand are mentally projected in three different patterns around the body.

The word of power AD-ON-O-I, pronounced ADDD-OUUN-OUUU-EEE. is continuously repeated in the great voice.

In the meditations we spell the words of power first and then repeat them always following the rhythm of the heart-beat. This exercise should be practiced for five minutes twice a-day for about two weeks.

b. THE NUMBER FIVE EXERCISES ON THE LEVEL OF AWAKENING. The powers of the hand are projected clockwise over the five points of head, feet & hands to form a pentacle. The pattern must be guided till the energies flow the appropriate way on their own, increasing in velocity. Only after the vibrations and heat sensations are equally strong on all the points should the regular meditation start.

Before the purification-exercises of the water, the energies of the hand are projected clockwise through the five points of power, forming a circle. We should at the same time rotate the eyes in identical speed and direction.

In the purification of the fire each point becomes the center of an arch. The streams are mentally directed counter-clock-wise to weave a golden hued flower around us.

The number five exercises variously called seal of Solomon, pentacle, mystic powers in man, or clavis Solomonis are supreme tools and protectors of the adept. Whenever the number five comes up in religious books in any form such as five leafs of the lily, fingers, men, and stars, they refer to the activation and employment of the five energy centers of the body. All five-pointed religious designs of flowers, buildings and geometric forms have the same significance. The phrases: work of the hand, finger of God, leafs of the rose, shining face of Moses, and the washing of hands and feet of the high priest before entering holy places refer to various exercises of the pentacle.

Important as they are, the "powers of the feet" are hardly ever mentioned in the scriptures. They are "the feet on top of the darkness", "feet that bring water by treading the wheel," and "the two poles that carry the arch." These poles, so we are told, cannot be removed from the sanctuary.

In the New Testament Peter says, (John 13:6-10:) "Lord (wash) not my feet only, but also my hands and my head..." Jesus replys "He that is washed needeth not save to wash his feet..."

We are told how to place our feet in the various asanas of the yoga, in the stances of the freemasons and Bektashi ceremonies. The Sufi orders have very elaborate regulations concerning the movements of the feet during the dances, but the reasons for these commandments are not revealed.

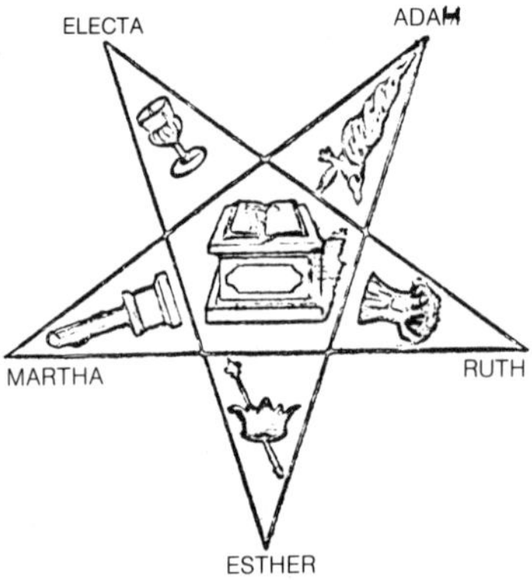

ORDER OF THE EASTERN STAR

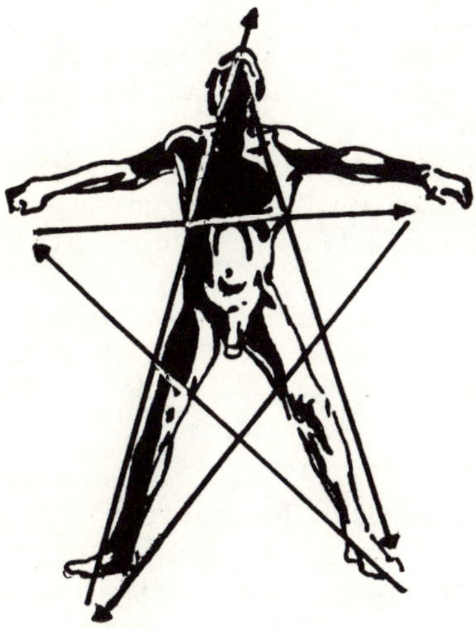

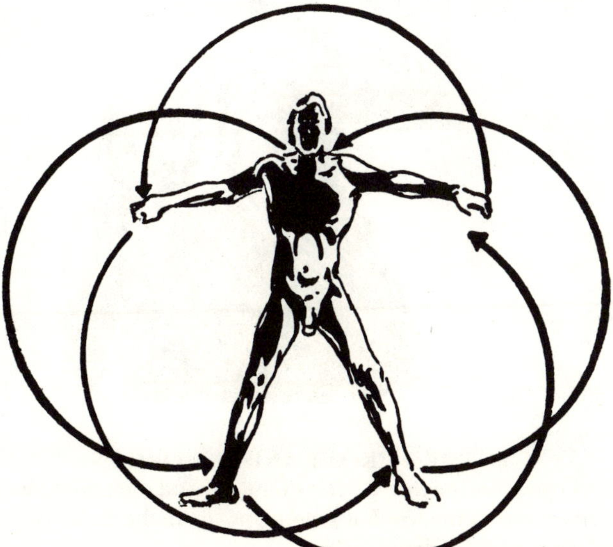

9. Code Number Seven

HAND OF TARA WITH THE SIGN OF POWER IN THE CENTER OF PALM

a. THE WAY OF THE RIGHT HAND, WATER PURIFICATION AND ACTIVATING

The first spiritual experiences come as subtle signals to the body. To understand their full significance you have to program yourself before the meditations to remember them when in the altered state. More about this discipline, called "questions asked and answers returned," later in this book.

Before the meditation, the second pentacle-exercise is made and only when all five points oscillate equally strongly do you place the left hand behind the head. This is to be its place during all the exercises of the activating.

The right hand will rest in turn on various parts of the body with the fingers held in the sign of the air or claw. The meditations can be made standing, sitting or laying down.

WORD OF POWER: ADONOI Repeated in the great voice

Twice a day, each time 25-30 minutes.

The energies of the hands activate hidden gate of perceptions on the body. The time needed to make each gate fully operative depends upon sensitivity, continence, time spend in studies, and regularity of meditations. If the exercises are interrupted for a few days only the benefit of the work may be lost.

THROAT GRIP

b. THE THROAT AND SEX ORGAN

The right hand embraces the throat. The thumb should rest about four inches below the ear. The vibrations of the word of power, spoken in the great voice, are projected mentally to the top of the spine.

All exercises are concluded by drawing the hand swiftly diagonally across the body to the right side just as if cutting with a knife. Before the next exercise rest the hand for a few seconds. Again making the sign of air, lay the hand alongside the sex-organ and guide the vibrations to the lowest end of the spine, a part that plays an important role in the work of the Cabalah.

In the commentary to Gen. 24:2, Rabbi Leon said:

> "Put, I pray thee, thy hand under my thigh..." This is symbolic of the foundation of the world, for this servant was destined to bring to life again the dweller in the dust, and to be made the messenger by the spirit from on high to restore *the spirits and souls* to their places, to the bodies that were dormant underneath the dust...
>
> Zohar 11, 181B

Before the actual meditations in the subsequent exercises, not only the five points, but all previously activated gates of perceptions have to be roused.

c. GATE OF THE HEART

The right hand in the sign of the claw is held on the left side of the breast, approximately four inches below the collarbone: "...we bend fingers of our right hand to catch the light of the lamp that is blessed..." (Zohar, 4, 207b).

At the end of the meditation the hand is drawn diagonally towards the end of the right rib cage.

d. SOLAR-PLEXUS AND EYE

Rest the right hand below the left rib cage in the sign of the claw. At the conclusion of this part of the meditation, the hand is drawn swiftly toward the right hip. After resting a few seconds, the hand is held above the right eye as if shielding from the sun. The thumb should lay on the temple. In conclusion, draw the hand horizontally to the right.

HEART GRIP

ROYAL ARCH SIGN

e. MASTERGRIP

Place the hand above the sex-organ meditate and move swiftly to the thigh. Rest. Hold the right hand above the crown of the head in the sign of the air with the index- and middle-finger bunched. In the conclusion both hands are lowered in three stages; pausing at the side of the head, the throat, and the breast for a moment.

HOLDING OF HANDS

The stances of the awakening and activating exercises are commonly shown on works of art as figures holding the right hand above the left. On the left hand rests either a symbol of the heart, fire, book etc. The right hand blesses the object. This gesture is emblematic for the position of the hands on the body at the stage of activating.

The vibrations of the words of power cause polarization in the subtle body. Biblical tèrms for the electro-magnetic energies of the body in their in-differentiated states are TOHU and BOHU (Gen. 1:2). The words are generally translated as "unformed and voice." The author believes that the terms should be understood as "confused and tangled," referring to the state of mind before the spirit of the elohim enters the "face of the deep," a term for the gates of higher perception.

The deceptively simple terms for the body energies after polarization are easily misunderstood. The positive male energy is called mercy, good, south, and the way of the right. The negative female energy, evil, justice, north, and the way of the left. Since the polarization takes place right at the beginning of the exercises, this occurence symbolizes the beginning of the human narrative in the Bible when Adam and Eve eat the fruit from the tree of good and evil. This will be explained later.

When the vibrations of the word ADONOI are felt all over the body, the work of awakening draws to an end. Currents of light weave a golden cloth in undulating movements over the body. The wonderful feelings of rest, peace, strength, and health that permeate the body after meditations were called the Shehinah by the cabalah and the bath of Mary by the mediaeval mystics.

MASONIC SIGN

AWAKENING OF THE HEART (EGYPT)

10. Code Number Seven

THE WAY OF THE LEFT HAND
OR THE PURIFICATION OF FIRE

In the stance of the fire-purification the upper left arm is held horizontally in line with the shoulder while the lower left arm points up at an angle of ninety degrees.

BOOK OF OPENING THE EYE (EGYPTIAN)

The left arm will remain in this "sign of the square" in all exercises of purification while the right hand, just as in the preceeding meditations, rests successively on various parts of the body. The hands now make the sign of fire.

WORD OF POWER:
AD-ON-O-I-EL-OH-EN-OU.

The pentacle exercise of the golden flower is made before the meditation to alert all points of perception.

The progress of the fire purification is signaled by colors, sounds and inspiration during the meditations. From the points of perceptions, vibrations issue that we may perceive as colors and/or as sounds. The purity of the colors seen with closed eyes indicates your progress in purifying your sense organs. The sound heard at that time replaces the "sound of the gavel in the east." This popping noise in the left ear was heard during the meditations on lower levels. As a signal to advance "at once" it was often heard more than once, depending on the intensity of concentration. The new sounds herald the removal of road-blocks.

In religious literature these sounds are called cymbals, silverbells, magic flutes, roar of the lion, but what phrase can describe the ineffable? According to ancient tradition each energy has a different vibration which we may hear as a harmonious sound or letter. Since there are thirty-two roads to wisdom, as the road to perfection was called, we encounter many sounds on our way.

PURIFICATION OF THE HEART

COMING OF THE RAVEN

The purification exercises of the fire begin with the holding the right hand on, or near the solar-plexus. After some time a black cloud is seen as signal for the start of the journey. At first the color appears only for some fleeting moments, an experience described as the coming of the raven, raven head, wings or dark cloud. This color is later seen for longer periods and will remain with us for years. Without the black cloud the proper work of purification cannot begin.

References to perception of this color are in the commentaries to Noah's tales, but they are detailed more fully in the sojourn of Israel in the wilderness. Just as this dark cloud guided Israel during the march, so will the color guide you now.

All colors of life are hidden in this black luminous cloud. And only after it lifts up from the heart can the serpent-fire be raised. Its energies spiral through the points of perception to destroy the negative precepts that hinder the work of perfection.

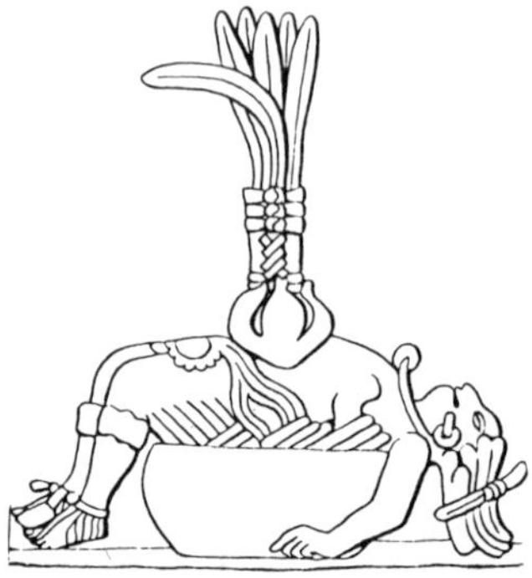

THE OPENING OF THE SENSE ORGAN ON THE SOLAR PLEXUS (MAYAN)

Each color that appears after the black cloud is lifted up from the heart comes from one specific point of perception. On the throat the color is royal blue that will change to bright green when the hand rests over the heart zone. With the blue comes clairaudience and the green brings the gift of clairvoyancy that allows you to perceive the aura of living matter. The green will change to white with the purification of the eye and the mastergrip transforms the white at measured intervals into a brilliant deep red. At the end of the process the whole body is clothed in a brilliant white light with blue fringes.

The appearance of the royal blue signals coming success in your endeavor. It is the color of the six covered wagons (Numb. VIII) in the wilderness. They are covered because the six gates of perception are not yet open and cannot perceive the full light from the crown.

The commentaries in the Midrash Rabbah that mention the different colors of the altarcloth refer to the color perceptions coming from the heart. Sacrifices at the altar signify the surrender of habits dear to the heart. Gluttony, lust, greed, desires, fear, curiosity, suspicion, lying, anxiety, and many others are to be sacrificed. Burnt offerings signify the fire that destroys all habits, weave offering are the spirits that put an end to hostility, while the offerings of libation quench desires, curiosity and anxiety.

Only after sins are expiated through these three sacrifices can peace offerings be made. When this has been done, you will be at peace with yourself and can enjoy the benefits of the work of perfection... You partake of the best part of the sacrifices ":you have achieved purity through sacrifices and offerings."

The blood of the sacrificial animal "is sprinkled on and above the altar, (your heart) on the cloth of the officiating priest and some drops are put on the tip of the right thumb, earlobe and the big right toe of Aaron the priest..." These are terminal points of the energy-streams of water that now flow without restraint through the body.

These are only a few of the recondite teachings of the oral tradition. Much more is hidden in the description of the sacrifices in the temple that belong to still higher grades.

The eradication of greed, fear, and other emotions are the sacrifices prescribed to produce mystic progress and the acceptance of the law of God, the offerings. The variety of material offerings (peace, meal) the flour, oil, birds, are symbols for good deeds for calling upon the name of the Lord, and for teaching the law. The cabalists say, "if we do not make good deeds, pray and teach, we are like a hard griddle. In commemoration of the time when we were a "hard griddle" we eat passover bread without yeast, the brittle mazzoth.

The terms for the spiritual body are: The mount, the building (ha-Bait), tent, the temple, the sanctum-sanctorum, the house of God, the tabernacles and the points of the compass.

The finishing gestures of the exercises are "the covenants" or spiritual "circumcision." Sepher Jezira, VI:16 "... the Lord gave the token of the covenant into Abraham's *hands*; that is the tongue and the circumcision between the thigh..."

The covenant of the circumcision is not a physical, but a spiritual act and the place of the sex organ is called "the foundation of the world" or "the gate of heaven" in the scriptures.

The critical moment that occurs during the spiritual circumcision is illustrated by tales in which the culture heroes are wounded near the organ of sex they get struck by a spear in lower parts of the body like Christ, or struck through the sex organ like King Gournemanz in the Grail-legends. When Noah left the ark, a lion struck and maimed him in the organ. The Pharaoh Neho was also wounded by a lion when he attempted to sit on King Solomon's throne. Moses had to be circumcised on his way back to Egypt in the night, after God attempted to kill him. Jacob was struck in the thigh while wrestling with an angel "in the night."

11. Code Number Twelve

The student cannot advance on the road to perfection without command over mind, emotions, and some bodily functions. These functions, called the "twelve common" are sight, hearing, breathing, speaking, eating, sex drive, movements, work, happiness, meditation (prayer), sleep, and anger. They should not be repressed but made to help you in your endeavors.

The twelve is a code number that stands for incompatible human tendencies. Many confrontations dissolve eventually in a unification of purpose, but not their identities. The diverse encounters of the "twelve common" are portrayed metaphorically in the tales of Jacob's sons, the sojourn of the tribes in the wilderness, apostles of Christ, of Imams of Ali, consorts of Texcatlipoca, Lords of the Katun in the books of Chilam Balam, and the star-constellations in astrology (MAZAL).

In literature as well as in works of art confrontation with these "twelve common" is presented in awkward ways and inconsequence easily misrepresented as when the manipulations of sex energy are portrayed as infidelity, masturbation, phallic worship, or parts of fertility rites.

The purpose of the cabalistic, Zen and Tantric exercises is to utilize the sex energies to recover, purify, and elevate the self. The cognomen for this process are mysterium conunctionis the barren woman conceiving, immaculate conception, and lifting up the virgin from the dust.

You will become aware of the means and ways to control the functions during meditations by physical signals and noetic flashes. The physical experiences consist of involuntary changes of body stances during altered states of consciousness, instinctive movements during prayers, unusual impulses, nervous spasms, streams of heat on the body, changes in the vibriaton on the points of perception and the rhythms of breathing. The meaning of these signals are by no means obvious. To discover them, you must be alert during meditation, experimentation, and study. The methods of probing the signals are described in another part of the book.

In addition to the general explorations, each of the "twelve common" has to be studied separately. Breathing is far more than an in- and ex-haling. An ancient sage advised his disciples to breathe through the heels: this is not a metaphor. The feet are a source of extraordinary energies. Folklore and legends speak about culture heroes who could have been immortal except that for one small spot on the body, either on the heels, the sex organ; or the shoulder blades, that allowed him to be killed.

Before starting these exercises, you may have the desire to massage the eyes gently or roll the eyes in their socket, to swing them from side to side, and to press the palms over the eyes with the fingers resting on the forehead. All these actions activate a point of perception called the "third eye".

Like the well known Chinese statues of the monkeys that do not see, hear, or speak evil, so the hands are placed over the eyes to promote clairvoyancy, over the ears for clairaudiency, and over the lips for wisdom. You may have noticed that while listening attentively, we often lay our fingers on the lips; this for a good reason. The Indian yogis hold their hands on the face in the exercise of closing the five apertures in the yony-mudra.

In our task to purify and perfect the self, the meditations help only if we observe, comtemplate and follow the directions that these seemingly unimportant common reactions convey.

WORK OF PERFECTION

12. Code Number Ten

THE WORK OF PERFECTION[1]*

In these meditations both hands are held now with identical signs on the places where only the right hand was used before. On these places, on and above the head, the sign of fire is made. On the breast the sign of air, and on all places below the navel, the sign of water is appropriate. The list gives the appropriate name of God used for each point on the body as word of power. The colors should come to awareness while concentrating on these locations. The energies that emanate from the higher sense

*Commentaries and Abstracts will be found at the back of the book.

organs are given names under the heading "signification". List names are inadequate to describe creative energies.

MASONIC STANCE

Body	Name & Translation	Name of God	Signification	Final Color
Feet	Malkuth Kingdom	Ad-On-O-I-Ha-Me-Leh	Continuity of Life	Gold
Sex Organ	Yesod-Ha-Olam Foundation	Ad-On-O-I Sha-Day	Creativity	Indigo
Right Knee	Hod, Majesty of Life	Ad-On-O-I Za-Va-Oth	Majesty Glory	Purple
Left Knee	Nezah Strength	Ihvh Za-Va-Oth	Strength Victory	Amber
Heart	Tifereth	Ad-On-O-I	Beauty	Deep Pink
Right Hand	Ḥesed Love	El-El-I-Yon	Love	Deep Purple
Left Hand	Din Justice	El-O-Him Gi-Bor	Justice	Orange
Throat	Binah Understanding	Ad-On-O-I El-O-He-Nu	Understanding	Blue
Eye	Hohma Wisdom	Ihvh	Wisdom	Red
Crown	Death Faith	Ihih	Peace	Brilliant White

THE AWAKENING

Let him who seeks, go on seeking
until he finds,
and when he finds
he will be disturbed
he will marvel
and rule over all

"What thy right hand will do,
let not they left hand know.
The Gospel according to Thomas

. . .and I saw in the right hand
of him that sat on the throne
a book written within
and on the back *SEALED WITH SEVEN SEALS
Revelation 5:1

13. Synopsis

The first exercises make your hand receptive to the existence and actions of hitherto unknown powers. During this work the perceptions, knowledge, and understanding of the true self increase and with the completion of this task we reach the first level of initiation.

14. The Exercises

In this book the basic occult teachings are presented in modern language. The study follows the text, the terms and the instructions of the "Book of Formation" and to keep it within the framework of European tradition, it is mainly embellished with quotations from the Bible and various classical commentaries.

The "Book of Formation" (Sefer Jezirah) had been a teacher's manual in ancient

---

*note that the book is sealed on the back

Jewish academies where students learned to relate *all* knowledge to the Creator. With the help of these laws of formation, they were taught how to master themselves, to master others, and eventually to master some forces of nature. These truly integrated inculcations trained priests, teachers, prophets, leaders and healers how to come to terms with the problems and forces of life that can not be conquered.

The neophytes learned primarily how to expand their perceptions by means of controllable exercises. To the casual reader these systems seem to differ greatly from one school to another due to the fact that the sages hid "the ways of god" behind fantastic terminologies, tales of God, sons of God, antagonists of man, and culture heroes.

The basic aim of those teachings and of all fundamental religions and occult schools can be summarized in the slogans: 1) know thyself first; 2) improve (purify); and 3) give thyself (sanctify, sacrifice) to humankind. This was the purpose of the initiation rites.

In the endeavor to know and understand the self, the sensory perceptions had to expand the awareness in order to guide the adept safely into higher realms, the way physical senses guide us in life. Once the students were able to perceive the higher forces, the initiation taught them how to control, direct, and repeat the phenomena that came with expanded perception. This made the initiates teachers, priests, healers and gave them dominion over others.

15. The Number Three *The Mothers*

To hide the teachings from the ignorant and guide only the initiated, systems of coded numbers were used, not only in the Cabalah, but in most sacred literature.

Of those ciphers the number three is emblematic for the powers that are supreme in the universe, known as the Genesis, the Law, and the Equilibrium of all created matter. These three forces regulate life and growth, influence fruitation and decay, i.e., they rule all existence from beginning to end. The cabalists call them "The Three Mothers." They are the powers of understanding, wisdom, and knowledge in the supernal grades beyond time and space.[2]

These powers come first to our awareness as vibrations that are produced in the hands by exercises of a kind of tuning-up process. They attract similar forces outside the body. One law decrees that supernal forces can respond only if there are similiar powers *active* within us. . . We will benefit from the vibrations only according to the amount of energy we can muster in our work.

The code of "the three" refers in *all* religions to the elements of life: fire, water, and air. They are presented in the Bible as culture heroes, generation mothers and angels. The cipher three in all its complexity is found in the global tales of the Flood represented as the three sons of Noah (the flood story in itself is a complete initiation parable). The patriarchs Abraham, Isaac, and Jacob are emblematic for the elements. That these three are really one is stated in many commentaries.[3]

Our soul has three levels that are emblematic for the three formative forces.

> Understanding, water is called Nefesh (anima):
> wisdom, the element air, is contained in the soul of the Ruaḥ;
> the spirit and the ultimate knowledge the crowning faith (animus) is the Neshama.

Thus the creation of man is mentioned trice (Gen. 1:27):

> ...so God created man in his own image=Neshama, Fire.
> in the image of God created He him=Ruah, Air
> Male and Female created He them...=Nefesh, Water.

These are the three levels of our existence: in God, in the soul, and in the body; and only the body was created male and female.[4]

As important as Moses is for the Jewish faith, he does not appear in the first part of cabalistic initiation. The trinity of Moses, Aaron, and their sister Miriam (Mar-Yam=Queen of the Sea, Goddess of Illusion, Maya, Maria etc.) belong to the next level. Symbols for the trinity on the highest level are David, Solomon, and the Messiah.

The number three has identical significance in other creeds; the eucharist, the archangels, and the Holy Trinity in Christianity. In Sufism, Hinduism, Shinto, and Buddhism, they are the three jewels, swords, metals (gold, silver and copper), three tools of worship, and a host of trinities, of culture heroes, gods, and higher spirits.

In Greek mythology we have the elements, graces, fates and, to mention only one of the many legends, the Maidens of the Garden of Hesperides. These three lovely maidens, with the guardian serpent Ladon, (ADON) and the figure of the culture hero Heracles (performing twelve labors that become thirteen) are centered around the fruit of the Tree in his Paradise with the Lord (Ladon) watching the garden.

The smoking of the holy pipe is the symbol for the "three" in American Indian's religions. The bowl represents the water (earth); the stem, the fire, and the 12 feathers of the eagle, the air.

In the lodges of the Freemasons, many symbols of the number three are emblematically displayed in the chairs, the greater and lesser lights, the working tools, the symbols of the officers, the two static pillars, and one that is not...

Therefore, when the number three is mentioned, we have to assume that this part of the scriptures is in some way a reference to one of the levels on which the supernal life forces act. But how do they act on the human being?

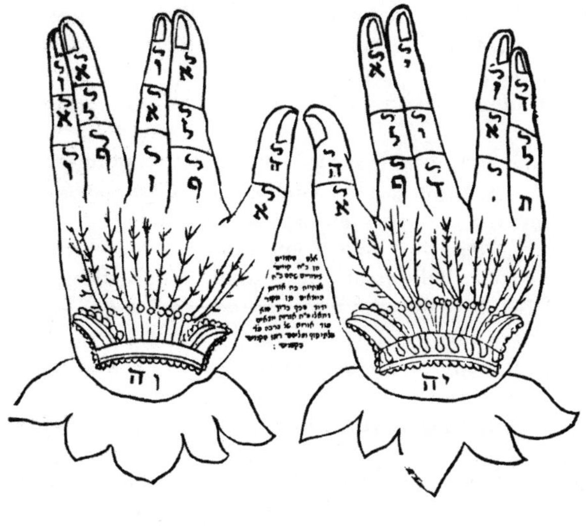

THE FIRST KEY

... opened one of the seals and I heard a noise of thunder one of the four beasts saying: "come and see." and I saw and beheld a white horse...

Revelation 6:1

16. Exercises of the Number Three

As insignificant as the exercises appear at first, they not only activate little-known powers, but are fundamental to all further stages of spiritual development. In the subsequent exercises, they are the keys to all we wish to achieve, to have, and to know.

The activating of the powers of the hands, also called "washing" or "enlivening" start with making "signs with the hands" (pointing the hand). All these exercises are described in the chapters of the spiritual exercises.

Once you become familiar with the "signs" you will realize that you have known them all your life.

The passages in the Scriptures that mention the action of the hands, such as "the work of the hand," "the right hand of God," "the purified hand," point to occult knowledge. *These are the keys, the best-kept secret of all religious teachings.*

In addition to the signs of the hands, "words of power" are used simultaneously.[5] These words are spoken with the great voice until the hands, the spine, and eventually the whole body is filled with the vibrations of "the word" in the tune-up process that was mentioned before. The great voice is an important term for words that are "spoken" in the throat, without the sound being heard. The vibratory forces of words spoken in this manner flow in streams of energies in and around the body, symbolically shown as quasi geometric forms; their movement must be directed by the student.

The three phases of preparatory work are: 1) the making of the signs; 2) the appropriate words of power; and 3) learning to direct and control the forces that become active in us.

Each of the three "elements" is meditated upon with a different "sign," word and pattern. The way the signs are made is emblematic in turn for vowels and letters that are the "word."

17. The Word

The higher energies cannot be released unless the gates of perception are awakened and cleared from negative forces that are called dust, stones, and uncleanliness in the scriptures. The work of purifying is done by leading the words of power with the right hand in an orderly and harmonious fashion into the body. Vibrations from the words of power cause the consciousness to expand. The author does not understand how the expansion takes place but the sensation feels like coming home and stepping into a well-known and beloved environment.

18. The Planning

Mephistopheles:	Take this key!
Faust:	That little thing?
Mephistopheles:	Take hold of it, not undervaluing
Faust:	It glows and shines! *Increases in my hand*
Mephistopheles:	How much 'tis worth thou soon shall understand
	the key will scent the true place 'mid all others
	So go with it. . . t'will lead you to the mothers.

Goethe, Faust, part 2,

The exercises of the vowels "i," "o," "a" will awake the three powers in the hands, provided you meditate regularly at least once a day for about 15-20 minutes. References to these actions of the hand are found in the Book of Splendour (1:34) together with the phrase: "the way of the right and left hand." Since you will hear this phrase quite often, it is better to consider some of its implications right at the beginning.

In order to have full control over the expansion of your perceptions, you have to hold the hands on several places of the body and beyond the body in a ver y strict order. It is of greatest importance that *only* the right hand be used. The left hand becomes active on higher levels and eventually both hands will be used. The rigid observance of these regulations is necessary *so that we do not loose control over our work.*

The work on the three levels is known as the left, the right, and the middle path (the path of Abraham, Isaac and Jacob).

Modern occult writers speak of the roads of white and black magic only, turning a highly complex field into a slogan and so making it possible for the dogma of the duality, which the serpent had introduced long ago, to come back. Cabalah teaches us that between the left and the right way, a third power holds the balance. This is in accordance with the occult law of equilibrium.

The planning of these exercises goes by stages. Inner signals will inform you when you are ready for the next level.

The formative life forces in the hands become active through these exercises. However, when planning the exercises, we should confine the work to the correct signs and words of power. In the beginning it is dangerous to do more. Later we will have to experiment. Through the exercises the hands become able to heal and bless. They should "become the working tools of the adept." In different faiths such terms for the number three sign of the hands are: knife, wand, scepter, holy waterpot, three-pronged staff, sword, plumbline, cup of grace, compass, bells, and levels.

When students begin to realize the field of the occult really is difficult to follow, invariably they ask, "Why should I go to so much trouble?" "What benefits will I have?" or "Will I be able to develop?"

When students ask these questions, they are usually already involved in the great science and the questions are really rethorical. Once we are involved in the study, we cannot turn back. Like Lot's wife, we cannot stop halfway between the old and the new life.

Once the effects of the exercises have been realized, you should plan research projects, in order to satisfy yourself that the stances and signs were not haphazardly given. We have to discover that the Cabalah is a real science.

The experiments should be comparatively simple at the beginning. Try taking the sign of the "i" and use the vowel "a" (mah), likewise can you take the stance of the "a" and experiment with the positions of the palms; for instance left palm facing up, right palm down, then reverse the palms to find which one of the positions gives you the feeling of being just right. These positions should be tried more than once. You then can create your own "words of power" with the help of the list of the Hebrew letters.

For group experiments the students should try stances of the Mayor Arcanas from the tarot cards. The words of power used for such experiments should include the vowel "i" for any signs of hand, held on or above the head. If the hands are held between the throat and the navel, the vowel is "a" and further below, the vowel 'ou' is used.

STANCE OF THE PENTACLE: RIGHT HAND IN FIRE SIGN, THE LEFT IN THE SIGN OF WATER

The planning of a full course has to consist of 1) prayer and contemplations, 2) regular exercises each day, if possible at the same hour, and later on experiments, 3) study of the Bible and its *classical* commentaries.

The reason for intense study is that the mind has to stay rooted in logic. You must analyze all matters of the occult as objectively as possible, never accepting any statements from anyone without testing their worth. If you should decide to develop your higher perceptions, you will have to abandon a number of precepts about the reality that you have cherished all your life. In order to keep the vital sense of orientation in the various sets of realities that exist side by side, learn to probe experiences form all angles to preserve a asense of humor at the same time. Following the reasoning methods of the sages, you learn to approach those spiritual lights in the correct way.

19. ESP Means Expanded Sensory Perception

In the search for lost meditation exercises the author experimented with the name of God, Elohim, as a word of power. In one of these sessions, quite unexpected most brilliant flash of light appeared before his closed eyes.

In Jerusalem in 1944 one of the few contemporary cabalists mentioned a bright, white light as one of the first experiences the student can have. "This light," he said, "is the light of the Lord, going through the Garden of Eden at midnight. . . to disport himself with the Righteous. . ."

This flash of white light is usually the first signal that you are on the right way. It is the carrot dangling before the nose of the donkey.

From the beginnning of the meditation you can *feel* some changes in you and your surroundings. You will *feel* that different emotional and spiritual realities exist in us. You will *see* colors, lights, forms, and faces with your eyes closed. The other senses will also register new sensations from time to time that are the beginning of E.S.P.

A bridge of a special kind is formed by our emotions. Feelings more than other faculties oscillate between the different levels of awareness and as a result precognitive perception become part of your life. The student will develop greater awareness of the feelings of others, of their fears, problems, and desires grows. Hand in hand the realization of the continuous stream of the messages that are relayed by all parts of the body will come. The eyes, the legs, the stances of the hands—all tell us new tales.

You will become aware of what is good or detrimental to your health. The sounds of animals convey messages, the plants and even so-called inanimate objects will teach you new language. In line with this, an appreciation of art, especially of music, poetry, and paintings grows, until the whole world shines in the beauty of the first day of creation. The working of the mind accelerates in many wonderful, exciting ways until suddenly you know that you can do anything you want to do. You can become whatever you want. Nothing that is not ultimately beneficial and necessary can happen to you.

This is what the rabbis meant in the commentaries, "Life and Death are in your own hand." They compared life to a bird in the hand of the hunter, whom a man met and asked him, "is this bird dead or alive?" "If you wish, it is alive, and if you wish, it is dead," was the reply.

20. New Awareness

A rather difficult question is how to decide for youself if an experience is really esoteric? How are esoteric phenomena experienced and their messages decoded?

The author found this to bè a good rule for judging the genuiness of an experience: if a phenomenon can be explained by any reasonable method, by common sense or by the rules of logic and psychology, it is *not* esoteric. Truly esoteric experiences come unexpectedly find us unprepared, and clarify hidden points of esoteric doctrines.

Symbols, tales, sounds, sights, and movements of occult pheonomena come in a great variety of ways. If we fail to utilize these experiences, if we do not study the meaning of such happenings and do not integrate them into our understanding, or if we reject them, we have lost an opportunity to progress. Each occurence is in a sense unique and should not be taken for granted.

Visual experiences can come when the eyes are open or closed. They may appear in front or on the side of your vision at an angle of 45, 90 or 180 degrees. When human figures appear, special attention should be given to the style of the costumes, hair and foot wear. However, understand that you will not see them in the conventional manner.

One occasionally sees auras. They will not necessarily follow the forms of the body, but may look like pyramids, pillars, or shells. During a prayer, a perfect aura looks somewhat like the Hagia Sophia in Istanbul with the supplications streaming up like the minarets.

HAGIA SOPHIA MEANS "HOLY WISDOM"

The colors of the auras can change from one moment to another, as can their forms. During meditations or even afterwards hearing plays strange tricks. You may hear whistling thunder, bells, or the roaring of lions. You may hear whole sentences, harmonious sounds, or even long compositions. This does not mean that suddenly you have become a composer, but you are receivers and/or a conductor of the music that is in each of us and yet not of us. What we receive and conduct comes from eternally existing harmonies of force-fields in and around us.

Accordings to legends, "the sound of the gavel in the East" was heard when King Solomon laid the first foundation stone of the temple. Other legends say that this sound is heard all over the world when the foundations of the inner temple are laid. The phenomenon is a sound in the left ear for men & the right ear for women, indicating that the meditation exercises are being correctly done.

"The catalytic exteriorization phenomena" (Jung) is a term for the bangs, knocks, and creaking of wood which come seemingly from somewhere in the room disturbing contemplation, exercises, or occult discussion. You should ignore them.

Feelings and thoughts can resemble physical experiences during meditations: peace can come as an essence, filling the whole body with a tranquil power. The light that comes during prayers becomes a protective shield. Fears come in human or subhuman form. The presence of powers and entities, the nearness of invisible friends and helpers seem to be very real.

Vibrations indicate the presence of formative powers; they are heralded by temperature changes in the body. Vibratory streams, resembling energy, flow over the body in different directions and electrical sparks fly from the fingertips. Even when you do not see them, you hear them.

When you no longer feel the body, when your hands seem to be pressed down or tremendously enlarged and extremely powerful, when you float above the ground, see your body below you, or suddenly find yourself in changed surroundings, you are experiencing the most common of all experiences, an out-of-body sensation.

> Sinai desert, 1937: After lunch we had to rest in the oppressive heat of the desert. The monotony of the wilderness, heat of the day and absolute quietness lulled the senses to rest and I found myself suddenly flying at tremendous speed through the air. Crossing a mountaneous area I felt exhilarated in an indescribably joy. Flying to my apartment in Jerusalem I found nothing unusual to pass through the narrow iron grates that protected the window and through it's glass panes. However, as sudden as I had come, I was pulled back into my body as if drawn by an elastic cord. I saw at all times the topography of the desert, as if flying in an exceedingly fast plane. Not like a dream.

After this experience the author made repeatedly out-of-body experiments. Passing through walls or closed doors was pure fun and only once did he imagine that he had died. He saw himself motionless on the bed. At this moment he began to worry because he could not remember the prayer to be recited at this moment.

To make out-of-body exercises, use the stance of the grand hail sign. Lay flat on the back without cushion. Hold both hands in a square, repeating AD-ON-OI.

Out-of-body visits to distant places can be scientifically checked, provided the targets are not well-known landmarks or familar to researchers and observers.

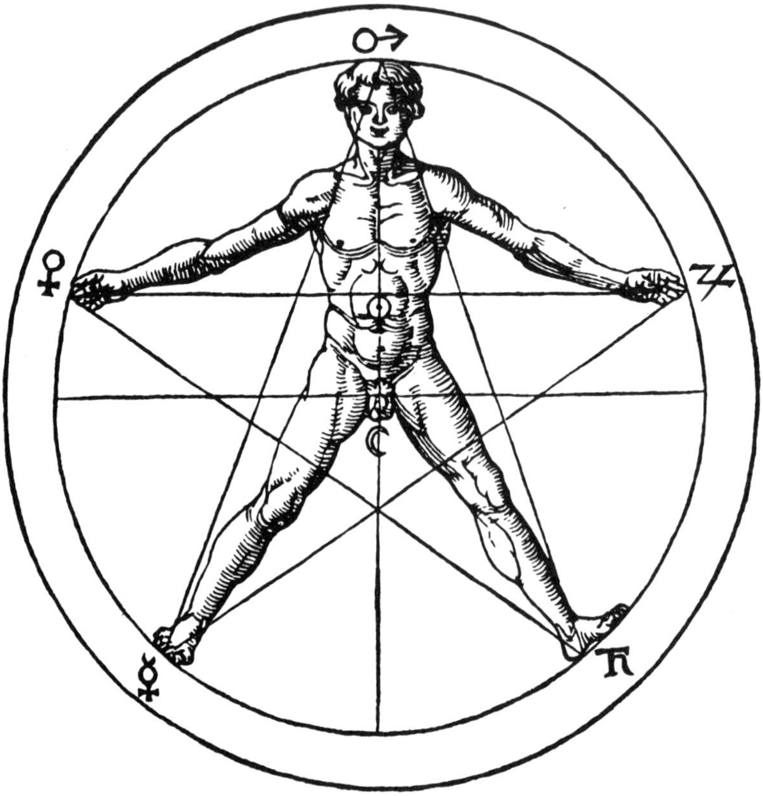

MEDIEVAL MAGICAL KEY

THE SECOND KEY

...He opened the second seal
I heard the second beast say:
come and see
and there went out another horse
that was red...

Revelation, 6:3-4

21. Number Five *King Solomon's Seal*

...that which made man man, is three letters and five points that which made the world, the world is three letters and five points
The son of Ethem, while he was ruler left his throne and crown.
That which made Ethem, Ethem is three letters and five points.
A Thurabi, that which made ten thousand worlds in one breath
That which made the worlds, the *worlds is three letters and five points*

quoted by J.K. Birge: The Order of the
Bektashi Darvishes, Istanbul Konservatori
Nesriyati Bektasi Neferserli 11:224

The number five is the cipher for the power centres: of the hands, the feet, and the head. These five points have to become active before you can begin the work of perfection.

There are strange secrets hidden in the seal of Solomon, who is represented in many designs and phrases as: the five points of mystical power, the pentacles, pentagramma, the gates of salvation, the cups of salvation, the strong leaves of the lily, the five helpers, and the points of the Gevurah (strength). The designs show a man standing in a five pointed star.

...Elohim representing the five strong leaves that surround the lily, symbolic of the five ways of salvation which are the "five gates." This is alluded to in the verse:

HAND OF POWER (ROMAN CATHOLIC) WITH CHRIST CHILD AS KING; HIS PARENTS AND GRANDPARENTS

> "I will lift up the cup of salvation" (Ps. CXVI. 13) This is the "cup of benediction" which has to be raised by five fingers and no more...
>
> Zohar, Prologue

The references to these points are in Sefer Jezirah 1:8: "The five against the five" and in Zohar III:35: "The supernal ark standing between the five."

In other faiths the emblems for the five points are the stigmatas of Christ, all pentacles, cross-bars, the Jerusalem, and the St. Andrew's Cross. The lotus flowers, eyes, and protuberances on hands, feet, and foreheads marks the points of power on pictures and statues of Oriental, Indian, and Tibetan divinities. The Masons call them the five points of fellowship and the Moslems, the hand of Fatimah el-Sahra, the daughter of Mohammad. Number five stances are familiar to all that have watched classical Javanese temple dances. Far less elaborate and more ecstatic are the dances of

FIVE POINTS IN MASONRY

WHIRLING DARVISH

FIVE POINTS ON THE CROSS

the Hassidim and the various Darvish sects. In these the dancers start solemnly and slowly accelerating to fast movements. Words they utter as they dance are repeated faster and louder in time with the speed of the dance. The Sufis use the words "Allah" (God) or "Hou" (He) as words of power, the Hassidim "Attah" (You) "Hou" (He) and "Adonoi."

The number five stance does not only give special powers all through the work of perfection, but when "danced" will protect the neophyte. In ceremonial magic, the Seal of Solomon becomes the most potent weapon against alien forces *in us.*

22. Summary

The phenoma that occur at the beginning of the work of perfection, including the powers of your hands, are not unique manifestations of any kind. They are not dispensations or special messages from supernal powers; they are life forces that are active in you, as they are in all living beings and guide your development just as the rain, the wind, and the sun make a plant grow. These forces will aid you in the unfolding and fruition of spiritual knowledge, wisdom, and understanding, provided you are attuned to them.

How these life forces act within the laws of creation and formation has to be experienced to be understood. To this end you have to awake and purify the higher sense perceptions that are as yet inactive.

ACTIVATING

"His disciples said to him:
is circumcision good or not?"

"He said to them:...
The true circumcision in spirit
Is good in every way."

Gospel according to Thomas

23. Numbers Forty-Nine and Fifty

Only when the palms of the hands, soles of the feet, and the center of the forehead vibrate strongly, can the spiritual sense-centers be aroused in the correct way. The existence of these gates of spiritual perception was a well kept secret for a long time. What they are and how they function is the content of the next chapters.

On our body are forty-nine such organs or, as they are counted in ancient documents, seven times seven.[6] One more organ exists about which very little is said in the books, which brings the archetypical number up to fifty. This is what the two numbers mean: the number forty-nine stands for the successful expansion of self-awareness that leads to complete understanding, while the mastering of the self is expressed by the number fifty.

24. The Sacred Seven

The exercises that activate the major gates of spiritual sense-perceptions awake by their quickening the whole body. You will become aware of the existence of these organs through vibrations that will well up within you in the most surprising places and at odd times. You may for instance awake in the middle of the night, long after meditation, to find yourself in an altered state of consciousness with the sense organs vibrating harmoniously, by a state that makes it possible for you to meditate (pray) during dreams and sleep.

One rule that must be obeyed is to meditate each day, possibly twice a day and always at the same hour. Also; lead these powers into the body in strict sequences. But most important of all, *the right hand* does the work of awakening, never the left.

Although the seven major gates are not really in the physical body, you will become aware of them through physical sensations at first; they are felt all along the body, from the soles of the feet to the knees and from the "end of the trunk," along the spine to the top of the head.

The emblems, names, and placements of the points of awareness are shown on the Tree of Life, the body of Adam Kadmon (the first Adam), and a host of various other schematic designs. They will be discussed in the chapter of the Elohim.

The Zohar (1.15) the holy book of the cabalist uses the term: "the backside of God," the Revelations: "the back of the book with the seven seals."[7]

When the perceptive organs are aroused, they alert the awareness to signals that had always been received but were not noticed or probed. In the following part of the work of purification, you will become aware of your real self and know how much more work is needed before you can go the way of perfection. These are the steps you have yet to take: the awakening of the awareness to the potentialities of the self, the purification of the perceptions, and the perfection of the self.

In the words of the Cabalah the work on the gates of perceptions changes death to life, devastation to creativity, and strife turns to peace, folly becomes wisdom, poverty changes to wealth, ugliness is transformed into beauty. The adept is freed from the slavery of the self. You become the master of your own fate. With the seven gates awakened and purified, you have gone through "the twice seven," "the seven doubles," or the fourteen stations.[8]

Of all the symbols of the seven, the Star of David and the seven armed candlestick (Menorah) need special consideration. These two symbols, are the keys to Isaac's conception and birth. Once this is understood, you will realize that the tales of the immaculate conceptions and births in all religions deal not with a physical but a spiritual phenomena: in the conception and birth, the Father represents the body, the Virgin Mother, the soul, and the Child, the spirit of God in everybody.[9]

25. Superstition

There is a belief in cabalistic circles that changing a name by adding a letter from God's name (the Shem-Ha-Mephorash) will make the bearer wiser, healthier or more wealthy, depending on the choice of letters. The letters of power in God's name H-O-I-A, can be added to a name or exchange with other letters.

> ...To nullify the decree of evil
> R. Huna said in R. Joseph name:
> Change the name and make good deeds...
>
> Midrash Rabbah, Bereshit, XLIV, 12

The number seven, sacred in most faiths, is mentioned about 500 times in the Bible. In Christianity, the Gospel of St. Matthew begins with three lists of fourteen culture heroes.

In the miracle of Canaan Jesus says: "...Woman...my time is not yet come..." and when his time came, he went through the fourteen stations of the Cross.

These numbers are part of several miracles on the shores of Galilea. They are described in Beatitudes, and at greater length in the Book of Initiations, "The apocalypse of St. John." Here the spiritual sense centers are symbolized as spirits, angels, churches, books of seven seals, thunderclaps, heads, eyes, horns, candles, and candlesticks. Most of these names are paired to make them the "seven doubles."[10]

In Shin-to, fourteen divinities came from the thigh of Izinami (Thigh of Jacob). The body of the slain Osiris is cut into fourteen pieces. There are also fourteen formulas of

OSIRIS RESURRECTED
THE 13 SERPENTS AND THE HAWK ABOVE REPRESENT THE CODE NUMBER 14. HIS SOUL (ISIS HOLDS HIM) AND HIS FOUR CHILDREN (STANDING ON AN OPEN LOTUS) ARE EMBLEMATIC OF THE PERFECTED BODY.

power in the Holy Book of the Moslems, "The Koran" and fourteen principal nadis (sounds) in Hinduism.

In Gnosticism, the spiritual sense centers were regarded as constantly active organs of lower desires that were loosely arranged in sets of seven, depending upon the sectarian pecularities, such a theft, slander, violence, ignorance, evil, rage, adultery, self-pity, grief, etc. These lists of misery were balanced with equally unorganized bands of seven angels that represented "words of power." In the manuscripts the angels Uriel, Raphael, Michael, Sariel, Gabriel, and Samuel represent the upper hierarchy of the forces of God.

26. Expansion of Perceptions

No attempts should be made to speed up your progress through the schedule of exercises for possible faster aquisition of psychic abilities. Sudden advances in this strange field can cause dangers far beyond control. Patience is needed to adjust to new ideas, changing values, and clearer understanding of other realities that exist in the self. If a permanent bridge is not established between the levels of consciousness, the self will fragment.

The safe expansion of awareness depends therefore on strict disciplines, study, timing, and the proper order of the exercises. The effects of a sudden awakening would be like a blind person's suddenly gaining full vision when stranded on a traffic island in a very busy intersection.

In groping ways characterised by all first experiences, sensory perceptions expand naturally and increase the desires to know and learn more about the hidden self. There comes to the fore the desire to understand more just for the sake of understanding and you will begin to long for these experiences that bring you knowledge and wisdom.

Only one organ should be awakened at a time, and the forces of number three and five have to be activated for each "grip" and word separately. Because the amount of time needed for each of the exercises depend upon the sensitivity of the perception and the intensity of concentration (not to speak about those who have psychic abilities) no time tables can really be given. Some information is in Zohar II, 7a-9a; other hints of the time needed are in the fourteen alphabetizing composition (acrostics) of the Psalms, Proverbs, etc. In the Koran we find at the beginning of certain Suras (2, 3, 4, etc.) after the opening phrase a number of letters that are used as words of power by the Sufis. The number of verses in these chapters gives the approximate number of days for each exercise. The twenty-two chapters of the Revelation of St. John also have a time table. (note that twenty-two is also a cipher). The cabalists consider approximately three years is necessary for a good beginning and your whole life for the completion.

CAUTION:

In any of the following exercises should the vibrations of the serpentfire (Kundalini) become too strong, bend the head forward and brush with the right hand over the body, away from head and heart.

THE THIRD KEY

> ...He opened the third seal I heard the third beast say; COME AND SEE and I beheld a *black* horse...
>
> Revelation 6:5

27. The Secret of the Covenant

The first step to awaken and consolidate our formative energies is achieved with the throat grip in which the bio-energies converge in the region of the third cervical bone. This exercise is called the King placed on the Throne. The other is the circumcision.[12]

The center of the three generative forces is in the area of the sex organ and will, when aroused, send its forces through a variety of channels over the body. The union of the bio-energy and the generative forces is the mystical marriage at the end of the work of purification. At that time the immaculate birth takes place that is variously, "the Matrona Meeting the King" — "the King lifting the Virgin from the Dust" — "Uncle Welcomes the Sabbath Bride" (Dodi Likra-at Kala).

Now, the gesture with which the different grips are finished after each meditation look like cutting off, scratching, or ripping open parts of the body. For this reason they are phrased as: "slaughter, killing, sacrifices, mutilation", etc. and on works of art the grips are depicted by knives held in one hand and the place of the grip made with the other. Here again the pictures show far better the different actions of the right and left hand. For the cabalists the phrases: sacrifices in the temple, at the *door* of the tabernacle, or north, east, west or south of the *altar*..." refer not only to possible historical events, but to the various sacrifices of habits.

For mystics the destruction of all that stands between them and God becomes the foremost goal. These are the sacrifices of our animal (nature).[11]

However, at times these terms of the spiritual sacrifices were mistaken for actual human sacrifices by priests and layment with tragic consequences. They not only insisted upon the bloody massacres of beasts and human beings in order to pacify God, to atone for sin or to please local deities, but also with financial and political ends in mind. Human sacrifices, including the sacrifice of children to Moloh, self immolations, ceremonial stripping out hearts to molify the sun, nuns cutting off their breasts and frenzied self castrations were done under deteriorating religious conditions.

28. Trivial Terminologies

The complex codes mentioned in the second chapter, cannot be deciphered without a good knowledge of the Hebrew language, but because they are challenging, many students get involved in the work of gematria or absad. They overlook the simple phrases, words, and tales because they do not seem to have profound meaning and are comparatively easy to understand. *These trivial terms harbor the secret of the work.* There are also other words in the Bible that appear to be out of place or the errors of some scribe; these are the words we have to study.

In the Bible there is *not one letter*, thought, or tale that has not intrinsic value. I have learned that: 1) a letter written in the Hebrew Bible that is placed a little below or above the line, or is larger or smaller than the other letters, or that has three odd letters on the top of one letter forming a crown and other irregularities are guides to the oral tradition; 2) stories of the culture heroes that are seemingly trivial when taken in their historical connotation also carry a message from the oral tradition.

A few instances of trivial words: "donkey" is a symbol for the ignorant man, carrying his burden of existence without knowing and understanding its purpose and goal. And so, the driver of asses is the teacher. The initiate who has full control over the self is riding on a donkey. When entering Jerusalem on a white ass, he is the initiate arriving at the level of highest knowledge in full control over all his purified faculties.[13]

29. Other Trivial Tales

Just as the cabalists regarded the tales of Adam, Noah, Abraham, and other culture heroes not only as historical happenings but also as devices for the teachings of concealed wisdom, so are the introductions to many paragraphs in the Zohar also tales that indicate the levels of initiation, secrets of degree, work, and ceremonies of mystical significance. These frames are either topographical descriptions of Israel, stories of fictitious Rabbis, mystical figures going *the way*, climbing mountains, meeting strangers, driving or riding on donkeys, resting under trees, or encountering dangerous serpents. Such trivial tales are used in many other works to hide valuable material.

30. Numbers

Numbers are divine ideas expressed in their simplest forms and stand for creative and formative principles in the human being. For this reason they are of identical significance in all religions and give the initiate instant clues to the meaning of terms, passages, symbols, and artistic representations.

Not to be obvious, seven is identical in meaning to 70, 700, or the completely fantastic 700,000 myriads. Example: seventy men of the elder of Israel; Moses will study the Torah in 70 languages.

Example of Gematria:

"...Now what is the 'secret' (SOD) of the Lord? CIRCUMCISION..." (Midrash Rabbah, XLIX, 2)

S=sameh has the number value	60
O=vav has the number value	6
D=daleth has the number value	4
Circumcision=	70

The SOD (secret) is in the circumcision=70=7 points of perceptions.

a. ARCHETYPAL NUMBERS:

One=the highest comprehensive aspect of life
Two=the development of life, of flux and reflux that brought strife and death into the world
Three=the actions of the bio-energies, fire, water, and air on all levels
Four=the secrets of the charioth in man, i.e., his subtle body
Five=the Seal of Solomon, your magical powers
Six and Seven=The Gates of perceptions
Ten=the force-field, energies that are the essential components of life, basic forces of the universe
12=bodily functions
13=the control over the bodily functions
14=the main gates of awareness, awakened and purified
22=building stones of the world
32=ways of wisdom
40=purification or pollution of the self
49=completed expansion of the self
50=mastery of the law

31. Conclusion

The esoteric teachings in this book were cross cultural studies of terms, tales, codes and descriptions of mystical thinking and experiences.

The notes on comparative mysticism have been added to show that all creeds are identical in their basic teachings, differing mainly in terminologies.

The next parts contain sign posts that lead into higher levels of the concealed royal road. When entering this part of the study and participating in the exercises, neophytes must understand that esoteric teaching *will change them.* These changes will be from folly to wisdom, from poverty to wealth, and from death to life.

PURIFICATION

1) Wisdom hath buildeth her house
she hath hewn out her seven pillars
2) she hath killed her beasts;
she hath mingled her wine;
she hath also furnished her table.
5) Come, eat of my bread,
and drink the wine I have mingled
6) Forsake the foolish, and live;
and go the *way of understanding*.
10) The fear of the Lord
is the beginning of *wisdom*:
and the *knowledge* of the holy
is *understanding*.

Prov. 9

Blessed is the lion which the man eats,
and the lion becomes man;
and cursed is the man whom the lion eats,
and the lion comes into man.

The Gospel according to Thomas

THE FOURTH KEY:

> ...and I looked and behold a pale horse: and his name that sat on him was DEATH...
>
> Revelation 6:8

32. Law: To Know Yourself

> ...You must understand that it is very difficult to be sincere with yourself. A man is very much afraid of seeing the truth...
>
> Gurdjieff

When, after considering the various aspects of the cabalistic work, you have decided to enter the road of perfection, first you must investigate the self. Obviously you cannot perfect what is not comprehended. As soon as you begin to experience occult manifestations, you will realize that your former awareness of the ego was inadequate.

Once the experiences take place, they must be correctly interpreted.

Since the success of the cabalistic work depends upon understanding what occurs during meditations, the first task is to study the unfamiliar signals that well up during the meditation. Many of these signals appear to be meaningless, or insignificant, but they are of considerable importance. They come as *involuntary changes* in the postures of the stances or grips:

> Mrs. L. Santa Barbara, Sept. 17, 1974: Called for Immanuel in meditation and felt his presence like a violet cape around me. My left hand raised automatically to extend outwards, right hand went over the heart.

These involuntary movements during meditations are fascinating phenomena, they indicate that a posture is incorrectly applied, held too long, or had lost its occult value.

> Mrs. L., S. Barbara, Apr. 21: Right arm rose up automatically then left, in meditation. Spiral energies arose, loud rushing sounds in ears, sexual feelings, violet and dark blue shapes seen.

The different rhythms or sudden spurts in breathing, or occasionally fast moving glimpses of objects and actions have no relation to the subject matter of the meditation; they are signals to terminate the meditation, as are those sounds from not-existing telephones or door-bells ringing. Likewise will meaningless words sentences, or sounds interrupt the contemplation as do various reading-matters, scripts, hieroglyphs and tablets stop you if you indulge in useless, pleasant musing or get immersed in erotic thoughts.

> Mrs. L., Santa. Barbara, Sept. 10, 1974: Body felt magnetic tremors all over. Saw words, like on a tickertape, in a strange language running in front of my eyes, too fast to remember characters. Mrs. L. Jan. 29, 1975: Awoke at night to see grey tablet like clay with strange letters on it. Felt head pressure, body prickles.

Sometimes these signals come suddenly and powerfully; they may be completely strange, different from anything you know. You may be caught by surprise since their messages have neither obvious meanings nor are self explanatory at first.

However, if you fail to respond to these signals, if you do not ask questions, the communications will cease; or if you do not meditate regularly, the swiftness with which the replies come to questions that may not be fully formulated, make responding difficult, Yet, answers are returned, just as gifts from God come before we realize that we are in need of them.

When you discover how recondite true knowledge of the self is, you learn to ask pertinent questions and by this, your knowledge will deepen. The signals of the unconscious will become clearer, you can relate the phenomena of sounds, colors, movements, etc. to your meditation.

Which kind of exercise causes what phenomenon? What does the appearance of color mean? Are they showing the activities of sensing points or of mood or state of health? How do you find the answers? *By asking*, by being able to sink the questions into the unconscious, *answers are returned*. Do not forget this.

All that you perceive at this moment are phenomena that the triune powers produce in their myriad combinations. The various signals in their great variety serve one purpose only: *to guide you* and nothing else. They indicate whether your actions are in harmony with the self. This harmony is all that is necessary.

When the phenomena are agreeable, when the colors are pure, the sounds harmonious, and no fears interfer with meditation, you can be certain that you are on the right way. If the phenomena are not agreeable *you must question yourself.* The experiences during the meditations will be different for each student and when the preliminary tasks are done, you will reach new levels of consciousness. At this time, a dialogue with the deeper self should commence, in which you can investigate the hidden recesses of the mind. The dialogue, prepared beforehand, should include the problems that arose from the signals that came from the unconscious. . . In this way you will learn to utilize the powers that act in you on the deeper levels.

In order to solve the problems and questions that relate to the self, to the outer world and to explore the many significations of laws, tales, and emblems whose meaning has eluded us during the studies, you must learn to *project them as questions* to the unconscious when in altered states of consciousness thereby building a bridge between two worlds.

When studying comparative mysticism, we find that each school kept some teachings secret and revealed others. Luckily for us, we can fill in some informations lacking in one school from the teachings of others. In Sufism for instance, the systems of the stances and the utilization of "dreams" is openly discussed; in Yoga, the sensing points and serpent fire is taught; in the Kaula, the breathing techniques; while in the Cabalah the secrets of the vibrations of numbers, letters, and words are not considered to be occult. For this reason the study of different methods of meditations and occult systems is valuable.

One of the non-cabalistic meditations begins by relaxing the body till we are aware only of the working of the heart, the brain, and one connecting vessel. Nothing else! This is done by the time-consuming discipline of ordering the mind to relax each part of the body separately. For an experiment, I selected the "hou" and placed the hands above the sex organ. No response came till I got bored and stopped the exercise intending to sleep. Completely relaxed in body, mind, and emotions, the sensing point of the base of the spine, "the foundation" awoke at this moment for the first time and the fiery vibrations of the serpent-fire welled in spirals away from this center, to envelope a great part of the body. These strong vibrations cautioned me not to proceed any further at this time but to wait until further discipline had better prepared me for such experiences. The experience also taught me that reality extends far beyond body, mind, and emotions into unknown parts of the self, a little known part of our being that is powerful far beyond imagination.

> Mrs. L. Santa Barbara, Sept. 12, 1974: strong tremors in top half of left side of back. Felt whirling wheels in neck. Was doing MIH, MAH and WHO, all 3 positions at the time. In meditation saw an angel with its hands in a circle, heart glowing on the palms of the hands...
> Oct. 15. 1974: Dreamed I was given one robe after another by nuns, lamas and priests to try on. It began to rain in many colors with flashes of brilliant white light....

As she advanced, her meditations and dreams became meaningful and increasingly noetic.

> Dec. 4, 1974: Very depressed. Felt a tingling over the body like a healing force; went into deep meditation. Saw myself as a child, holding a tall man's hand. He showed me a bubbling pool and said: "those are your emotions, but that is not you." Then he showed me a complex of wires and said: "That is your mind, but that is not you" Then I saw a corpse, just bones and skin, and knew that was not me either. He told me to keep my mouth open and to breathe out from my lower stomach, but not to swallow the air. Then he gave me a tiny pearl saying it was my soul, my "self" and he put it in my heart to be polished to luster, grow and radiate the beauty of the creator. He said his name was "IMMANUEL."

Further advancing her recondite experiences became difficult to describe. When using the name IMMANU-EL (God with us) as word of power its vibrations led L. to truly mystical experiences. Geometric forms, numbers and symbols became now the language of her occult visions. She saw:

> "swirling luminous clouds overlapping and dissolving" and "six-sided harmonies in a fourth dimension."
> Oct. 18, 1975: In meditation a hawk appeared holding a scroll in his claw, which unrolled. The design was:  The message was: Center of the universe. Then a  square appeared, staying. The hawk spoke: all comes from within — spreading outward from the source — the dot."

In these attempts to penetrate the hidden parts of the self, the novice faces extremely potent forces. They have been called the powers of good and evil, but this phrase fails to convey their complexity. With expanded awareness, we encounter forces that have been called angels and devils, the choices of Hercules, or the forbidden fruit of the mythological tree of good and evil. Remember that they are most likely to come when

Oct 18. In meditation - a hawk appeared holding A scroll in his claw - .which unrolled the design was  The message was: center of the universe.

then a □ square appeared, staying. The hawk spoke " All comes from within - spreading outward from the source - the dot."

THE JOURNAL OF MRS. L.

the mind is at rest. What are these powers of good and evil? *Good is that which perfects the self, while evil is whatever stands in the way of perfection.* It's as simple as that. Once you realize that extent of devastation caused by ignoring or gratifying the negative sides of the self, you will understand a great deal more about your life. The evil disguised as logic,common sense, as stubborness, fear, or superiority complex, habits whether good or bad, hamper the understanding of the self. All the customary behaviors, because they seem the sensible things to do, are road blocks to the quest. Even meditation can hinder your progress when done routinely. These forces are difficult to conquer, since you have lived with them for a long time. When you fight them, they will change their disguise and become more subtle, more powerful, more vicious as you advance in the work.

The stories of the Exodus and the sojourn in the wilderness illustrate best the fight against negative forces at the time when the adept sojourns in the wilderness of the self.

Other faiths have other tales, but all have identical endings, whether they are Essenes, Buddhists, or Christians; only after fighting the evil inclinations for *forty* days, or years, did they reach their goal.

The dramatic stories of the slavery in Egypt, the Exodus till the death of Moses are cabalistic descriptions of the roadblocks set up by the self against the advance towards perfection. To make this clearer, I will explore some of the Biblical tales, terms, and phrases.

The forces that keep Israel in bondage are symbolized by the strange gods of Egypt, the despotic Pharaoh and the oppresive Egyptians. The phrases "strange god" or "strange woman" infer the erroneous concepts about religion and worship (of statues, pictures and stars). Pharoah represents the egotistic desires. The oppressive nation is the code phrase for social habits and the rules of society. The Exodus from Egypt represents the escape from the bondage of all these forces to be able to worship in the way that advances your progress. "Israel," as a term, stands for the state of perfection and means "striving for God, the Prince, or Son of God".

The seven groups of adversaries in the self are hatred, misfortune, poverty, slavery, sickness, fruitlessness, and death. Physical shortcomings that can never be completely overcome are called Amalek, Mo-ab, Baalam, and Balah. The ordinary habits and vices are represented by those animals that can be sacrificed at the altar (the heart); hidden addictions are the crawling things, the scorpions and the fiery snake that disappear as "Israel" advances.

Other adversaries are symbolized by individuals who rebelled against the Lord; envy and vaingloriousness, for instance, are Datan and Abihu who acted in matters of the deepest secrets without being prepared. In the incidents of groups, adversaries were represented by those who muttered against God or Moses; those who committed the unspeakable act of making the Golden Calf; and those who brought about the breaking of the tablets made by God which were replaced later with tablets made by Moses. Other tales symbolize the same obstacles in different ways; as the other shepherds, Yezer-rah, the devil, satan, Lilith also called Dalilah, the darkness of the soul, the queen of the night and the stones on top of the wells.

Because of its impact on the work, the last allegorical phrase needs to be examined in detail.

The culture heroes Abraham, Jacob, Moses, meet their future wives at the wells. Cabalistically that means that the body and soul become aware of each other for the first time on the sensing points. These wells enclosed by stones, that are guarded, or used by "other" shepherds (identical with "other" gods), is decoded to the sensing points are blocked by negative forces. Now, the stones that close the wells are rolled away, removed, or beaten with the rod of Aaron (by Aaron or Moses). With the identical rod, rocks are beaten to bring water. The bitter waters are made potable by the use of the same rod that had been used before by Jacob (Gen. 30/38) when he increased his flock by making them speckled and striped,

> ...he set the rods which he had piled before the flocks in the gutter of the watering troughs...
>
> Gen. 30/38

We all have this rod that can be turned into a serpent. It is in in the life force that flows up the spine. We all have to make it fit for the work of perfection. The waters from above, stand for the emanations of God, while the waters from below represent illusions. After the Israelites had passed through the Red Sea, when culture heroes emerge from the waters; whether above in or beyond the waters and whether in clouds, floods, or the sea, they had to go on a journey through the wilderness...for forty days or forty years, after which they became leaders or teachers. In all these tales the number forty is the cipher for *purification through water.*

> ...the rabbis say: "come and see all the miracles which God wrought for Israel. He wrought only through water...
>
> ...The rabbis say: "the law is compared to five things; water, wine, honey, milk, and oil...
>
> Midrash Deut., (Ekeb) III/8

The phrases "waters," "the oil flowing over the head of the high priest," "Noah's wine," and "the land where milk and honey flows," all stand for the reception of highest emanation.

The guides through the wilderness are Moses, who represents *wisdom* in pursuit of perfection, his brother Aaron who is the emblem for *knowledge* beset by desires fluctuating between highest inspiration and physical pleasures, and Miriam, their sister, who is the *understanding*. This triune principle of wisdom, knowledge, and understanding is the trinity of elements on the highest level.

The principle of wisdom (Moses) has the highest merit, since it can overcome egotistic desires at once, while knowledge (Aaron) frees the self more slowly from bondage of the negative forces by the gradual expansion of the awareness. The recapitulation (Deut. 2) of the stations and incidents during the sojourn in the wilderness are a coded resume of the work on the different degrees of the purifications, the perfection of the work, and its timetable. This summary has neither historical or geographic significance.

The quest, "to remove the stones from the wells," is contained in the twice seven stages of purification, it is outlined in the chapter on the sacred seven. These sensing points, are symbolized by the wells that supplied the water during the forty years in the wilderness. The rabbis say that only one well was with Israel all the time and went through all the stations with them. This well is mentioned forty times in the five books of Moses.

How do we purify the sensing points? The first two sensing points, the one on the throat and the one near the sex organ, have to be purified simultaneously. The progress in the work of purification of the point on the larynx is achieved by the following disciplines:

— to contemplate each day at least once (the rabbis said three times a night)
— to study holy books and their commentaries
— to live in harmony with the self and the world
— to control your conversation
— to devote time only to important tasks
— to relate all experiences and thoughts to life at large.

The point of the foundation on the sex-organ is blocked by egotism, lust, anger, vice, greed, delusions, pride, and envy. When the two points are vibrantly awake and purified, the other points have to be activated in order to keep the expanding awareness in equilibrium.

This is the outline of the study of the self, a task that can never case. Why not? Because the self will not cease to reveal more about itself while we advance in this task.

THE FIFTH KEY

> ...and when he had opened the fifth seal, I saw under the altar the souls that were slain for the word of God...and *white* robes were given unto everyone of them...
> Revelation 6:10-11

33. The Great Awakening

The identical rules, which are valid for all human beings throughout time and space, are enforced by ten forcefields (the sefirot of the Cabalah). They were the first emanations of God; to experience them is the highest goal of the cabalist. The scriptures reveal very little about them, but just as with the secret name of God, these forces manifest themselves in due time to those who work for their own perfection and who pray.

The first governing principle of these force fields is the law of the trinity. All references to the highest aspects of the three powers signify perfection and harmony that can be obtained only by keeping the influence of the ten forces in perfect balance. Neither knowledge, wisdom, nor understanding alone suffice to succeed; all three must rule as one.

During the work of perfection each of these elements will dominate all points of perception for a time, so that you will pass through water, fire, and air, in turn. This is a familiar phrase from the initiation stories. According to the textbooks, wisdom will rule the belly, knowledge the head, and understanding the breast during this part of the work and, at its termination, when we are patriarchs, they will be one. This must be kept in mind since the sequence of arousing the gates of perceptions has to proceed in the proper order so that balance is maintained. The point on the larynx, for instance, is ruled by fire, consequently, its forces naturally go upward while the point of the foundation that is enlivened at the same time is of the element, water, with forces going down. The balance is maintained by forcing the water up, the fire down, and awakening the heart to help balance the high flying spirit and the desires which are not yet purified.

The story of Adam and Eve is a dramatization of the law of the supernal knowledge that permits eating of all the fruits of the tree but not the fruit of *understanding* good and evil alone. When they did eat it, their eyes were opened, but they saw only themselves and not God. The story makes the point that knowledge was missing, they were imperfect, and God could not be with them in their imperfection.

34. About Signals and Symbols

Some of the signals that come from the unconscious are hardly noticed at first. The brain is not programmed to decode them automatically as it does the physical sensory perceptions. When the signals do reach the awareness, the mind does not care to distinguish between real messages and fraudulent ones because the fraudulent signals coming from the adverseries are considerably more alluring and pleasant than the real messages. For this reason, every impression must be analyzed each time it occurs since it comes from a highly labile part of the self.

After the awakening when these signals come more frequently, actions are taken during meditation to quicken the vibrations of the points. The actions are described in the scriptures as beating, rolling, opening, churning, etc. The expressions suggest, although not very successfully, what kind of procedures help during meditation. What they try to say is, that when one of the points begins to stir, the mind should increase its vibrations by exerting the power of the word, by beating the yet inert (rock) points with its vibrations (turning the wheels, churning the milk) until such time when the point will reveal its own peculiar rhythm and nature.

Of the many signals you will receive, the color sensations are the only reliable ones to guide you in the timing and the correct sequences of the awakening exercises.

The appearance of some very specific colors that you not so much see, but feel and think, are caused by vibrations in the sensing points. The progressive intensity and clarity of those vibrations change colors in regard to purity and hues, giving the clues to the progress of the work.

The first of these color impressions is the "thick darkness" that signals the start of the great work the author described in "code-number seven." As long as the "black, deeper than black" is not seen, that means as long as you don't behold your soul "face to face" the exercises have to be repeated.

When we eventually are wrapped in that luminious cloud, we can advance only after the "dark cloud" lifts. How else could we advance?

The cloud is coded in the Bible in various ways. One of them is "the black raven" that Noah sent out from the Ark but did not return and was seen feeding off the carcasses of the flood." Ravens are the emblems of cabalists, alchemists, nordic religions, and Rosicrucians.

Darkness over the faces of the water, the dark cloud over the altar, the little black sister, the Ethiopian woman of Moses, the Queen of Sheba, and the dark skin of Job are other code phrases for this signal.[14]

In other works the color impression has other names, such as "the skull, the darkness before dawn, putrification, a deep blackness at noon and the "unclean, deep blue" of the Tibetan.[15]

The dark colors dissipate during the course of the exercises. The greyish hue becomes burnt orange, eventually turning crimson. With more meditations the red becomes green.

> ...the fiery mass draws out from within itself a variety of colors. The first is a green color. When that color appears the fiery mass raises itself and plunges into the midst of the green color, occupying the inner part of it...

The green turns off-white (Noah's dove), after which all colors appear at once, the covenant of the rainbow is the code for this. When the many colors of the rainbow are seen, the heart region should be roused, since from this point, the powers will stream all over the body, "like the rays of the sun," is one of its emblems. A source of inner light, its awakening brings a beautiful blue to the awareness and a sound like the tinkling of silver bells (Miriam's cymbals) that is perceived not only in the ear.

The heart region, as the center is the holy of holies, the tent of meeting (where the soul consciously unites with the mind), the place of the mystical union, the chymical marriage, and the unification of the two triangles that form the universal symbol of the star of David. In addition to the heart, the center is also coded as the sun, and the year, all three symbols appearing in the Mayan, Hindu, Nordic, and Chinese, cultures as the escucheon for culture heroes.

All the numbers used in the scriptures relate in several ways to the sensing points. A sense organ is perceived as an oscillating unit with the appearance of flowers, wheels, or geometric designs in motion. The design is partitioned into segments that looks like petals or spokes, and the number of these segments in the design gives it its cipher number. Additional details about the intricate symbolism of sensing points can be found on the list of the number seven.

The cipher number of the heart center is the number six (six hundred, six myriards) and its multiples of twelve, eighteen, and twenty-four. Six of the twelve segments represent faculties that we can control and develop, while the others will unfold by themselves. The one that can be developed refer also to the six levels of the quest, emblematically described in the six formative days of the creation, and the six hundred years that Noah worked before the flood began.

The forces of the number twelve are the powers that perfect man, when controlled. The various tales, symbols, and commentaries connect the twelve princes of Israel who send six covered wagons drawn by twelve oxen (Num. 7:3) as an offering to the tabernacle with the forces that guard the heart. The rabbis said that the wagons were blue colored. Note that blue is the color of the opened heart.

35. Dreams, Sleep and Visions

The dreams balance the states of wakefulness and deep sleep. The content of the dreams influence the actions by day and relaxation during the night. When the work of perfection is carried into night, your dreams will change considerably. They will acquire more significance since their contents will deal mainly with the problems of the quest. They will become clearer, more vivid, and will be more easily remembered. You must learn to influence your dreams so that negative powers that plagued you during the sleep, become subdued. Remember that the negative powers enter the awareness only if you sincerely desire to advance. Once you become aware of them, you can begin the work of eliminating them.

As the influences of the negative desires decline, the dreams become precognitive and change eventually into visions.

The root of the word vision, comes from the time before the dispersion of Bab-el (door to God) and is read M-R=Mar (lord). Cabalistically, the root may be decoded as

the ruler over illusion, our soul, and is explained this way:
— The letter "M" is materia, water (mayim) or mother
— The letter "R" is the Ruler (Rosh), hero, or illusion.

This root M-R stands in many other languages for soul and vision.
— mirror of the self;
— mir (German)=myself
— mirar (Spanish)=to see
— Mar'h (Hebrew)=vision
— miru (Japanese)=see
— mirus (latin)=astonishing

Miracle, more, meri, Miriam, maria are other words containing this root. Visions are the language *of the soul and the means by which the spirit communicates with the awareness.*

When the problems of the daily life are taken to the level of sleep, they can be solved and the answer returned in dreams. At the level of development when you are fully conscious during the dreams, you can observe the negative forces and free yourself from the bondage of those powers to work (that is, pray and meditate) or help others during the night. You are now aware of the guidance of the real self that rules on this level.

According to oral tradition we have three souls; the lowest is the physical soul, Nefesh (water); at the next level, the emotional soul, called Ruah, (air or spirit) isn't fully awake in most people, while the superior soul, Neshamah (fire), has to be reborn. This, the highest and most precious part of the soul, lies in the dust. As the phrase goes, she must be lifted up to be united again with the king. Only Neshamah, the highest soul, is the true mirror of the self. The value of dreams depend upon which part of the soul is dominate at that time.[16]

In order to use the dreams and sleep for the work of perfection exercises must be made before falling asleep. The Talmud BERAḤOT advises the student to pray in bed, and have the head of the bed placed toward the north. Instead of becoming completely oblivious to the self, awareness can enter into an altered state of consciousness during which we learn to manipulate dreams.

In this state you can easily recognize and repel the attempt of the adverse powers to distract you from the work on the self.

The meaning of the masked, grotesque, or disturbing happenings during dreams, need not be analyzed, but faced by coping with the problems they try to create. In this way problems of the waking life dissipate.

You may, for instance, be chased by a fiend to the brink of an abyss in a dream; you are now fully aware of being in a dream-state and can signal your mind that a) you are dreaming; b) that you don't need to be afraid, since you can float down or jump across the abyss; and that c) you can terminate the dream or command a happy ending to it.

By this, knowing that you control the dream, the adverse powers are controlled and the unpleasant dreams will eventually stop, When you enable the awareness to help in your dreams, the awareness becomes a tool to divert the self from weaknesses that plagued you during the night. At a next step, the awareness becomes able to penetrate the world of sleep and you begin to make out-of-body travels during your sleep. At this stage as with the preceding one, the exercises, stances, gestures, and words can be put to work while mind and body rests. The lack of interference of the physical and intellectual facilities brings the subliminal experiences faster. They will become so clear that you can enter higher levels of awareness just like entering another room.

Nevertheless, this is only the beginning of the journey into the wonderland of sleep in which we see the self in its totality and are introduced to the "dark side of the moon".

A woman came to Rabbi Eleazar to have him interpret a dream in which she had seen a split beam. The Rabbi told her that she will have a baby boy, which happened. Again she had the identical dream and again she gave birth to a baby boy. However, when she had the dream a third time, the Rabbi was absent and disciples told her that her husband would die;

> . . .she began to cry. Rabbi Eleazar heard this and asked his disciples "why is this woman crying?" They answered "she came to inquire of you, but did not find you." He said to his disciples "what did she come to ask?" They informed him; and he there upon said to them: "You have killed a man; for it is written" and *it came to pass, as he interpreted it to us so it was.* (Gen XLI) And did not Rabbi Johanan say: "a dream follows its interpretation. . ."
>
> Midrash Rabah, Lamentations 1.1: 18

36. The Roar of the Lion and the Hum of the Dragon

At some time during the purification exercises the bio-energies will flow from the heels through various routes up the body. This flow cleans the sense centers. From then on your experiences, especially the lights and colors, become brighter and clearer: "You start to see, and hear" *the roar of the lion.*[18]

37. The Man Eats the Lion

Sound perceptions change. The silvery sound of the cooing of the dove is drowned out by a low rumbling noise emanating from the sex-organ, the foundation. The varied descriptions of this sound show how many expressions can be used for one phenomenon. To the author it sounds like the throbbing of drums, to others like the noise of an express train, the sound of a giant bow being strung or the growling of a wildcat that becomes the roar of the lion. Other descriptions are, the blast of the trumpet, the shout of the warrior in the camp, thunder, the shofar, the tubamirum of resurrection, and the hum of the dragon.

CONCLUSION OF THE PURIFICATION

The powers that expand the understanding, abilities, feelings, and concepts come from a spark of purest energy in us that the sages called the "flaming halfshekel from God." Other terms for this spark are "the small face," "Elohim," "the Power (Hand, Finger) of God" and "the Commandments." The letter I (Yod=Hand) and its number ten, "the five against the five," are emblems for the energy, as are the two pillars Yakhin and Boas at the entrance to the great temple. These are identical with the two tablets of the ten commandments on which the law was written by the Finger of God (it does not say "fingers" of God).

The work of purification is to become pure enough to receive the law of God.

You will use both hands in the second part of the purification exercises. The "five (fingers) really stand against the five" but the right hand remains in command to direct its benevolent energies to the sensing points in order to keep control over the five powers of the left hand. When, during this exercise, the fire ascends or decends beyond pre-established stations, although you will be pleased and fascinated by the experience, you should stop your meditation. Bend the head and the knees to contain the path of the fire and you can quiet the vibrations by brushing the right hand over the body. The signal to proceed is the "sound of the gavel" heard twice in the left or right ear.

Now you are ready to develop all the benefits of expanded sensory perceptions; clairvoyance-and-clairaudience, out-of-body experiences, precognition, and the gifts of healing. Your center, the hearth, had been described before. The other six points are:

a. THE CROWN OF THE HEAD, KETER, SUPERNAL KNOWLEDGE

Although you will feel some vibrations on the top of the head, during the first exercises this gateway to highest levels will open its full splendour only, ". . . when the oil of the law and the blessings of the Lord can rest there. . ." Remember, the blessings of the Lord can rest only on places of purity and fullness of life. The gateway opens, He comes as "the face of the sabbath and crown of the King. . ." The supernal forces bring rest and peace. This is the secret of the true sabbath.[19]

The crown, said Philo Judaeus, is not only the place where dominion reigns "when the slavery of the senses has terminated," but

> . . . He caused to rest therefore on the seventh day from all this work which he had made" (Gen. 11:2). This is as much as to say that God ceases moulding the masses that are mortal, whenever he begins to make those that are divine and in keeping with the number seven. . .
>
> Philo Judeaus, 88-129

In other cultures a vast array of works of art depict this hidden sense organ on the ceremonial headgears in a variety of designs combined with emblems of the number three. The most conventional symbols are halos, crowns, upright or reversed flowers (the rose, the lilies, and the lotus), feathers, thrones, and serpents. Far more difficult to decipher are the designs of ceremonial wigs and head decorations of Gods, kings, initiates, and noble men in the Mayan, Aztecs, Egyptian, indian and other Eastern religions, since they show the station, rank, and abilities of the figure, but the various tonsures, hairtufts and crests, and other hairstyles also represent this gate of perception. This is the mystical significance behind the scullcap traditionally worn by orthodox jews, certain catholic monks and the Pope.

b. WISDOM, ḤOḤMA

The second sense organ is the third eye, the mark of Cain on the forehead. The pylactery of the head (tephilei rosh) is emblematic for this place and consists of a little box filled with prayer scrolls. Just like the skullcap, the tephilei rosh has not only ceremonial meaning but reaches into the domain of the inner light ("fire") and has therefore the letter 'sh' as emblem on the outside (Esh=fire).

HEAD PHYLACTERIES

Thousands of tales, emblems, and poems hail the moment of awakening (the journey into the day, the light of the word) as the most glorious achievement on the road to perfection.

> ...Judah remarked "as indeed we find that a real blessing is associated with the opening of the eye (singular). Thus is written "open the eye" (Dan IX:18) that is, in order to bless.
>
> Zohar. V Naso: 147B

This sensing organ, freed from impurities, is capable to project desire, thoughts, and commands into any direction and, for this reason, the initiates are shown with rays of light streaming from the head (Moses). In other cultures, the emblems of the eye are feathers and wings on the head of Gods (Mercury, Sebek, Maat, Osiris, and Quetzalcoatl) and horns of Lucifer, the devil, Krampus, the unicorn and the culture heroes (who disguised as bulls will loose a horn during battle). Several African tribes carve square designs on the forehead of their religious statues that resemble the head phylacteries. Some traditional headbands and braided leather-thongs hold these symbols. The marks painted on the forehead, tatoos and welts caused by banging the head on the floor during prayers (as some orthodox Moslems do), all signs of the third eye.

In astrology, the eye is the moonsickle with its two points pointing upwards as an emblem for wisdom. In mythology and religions, female figures, emblems of the soul carry the moonsickle on the forehead or float over it; Mary, Isis, Io, Kali, or Venus are the carriers of wisdom (with the serpent or dragon beneath).

Just as Cain received a sign on the forehead to save him from being hurt ("...and the Lord set a sign for Cain..." Gen. 4:15; Abba Jose said: He made a horn grow out of him.) So the moonsickle on the forehead of Venus was the key to the abyss, and whosoever had this seal (Eosforos) could not be hurt. (See, Talmud Shab. 49a, Elisha and the Tephilin.)

c. UNDERSTANDING, BINAH

Greater understanding of the self comes with the purification of the organ near the third cervical bone, which is purified by the grip on the larynx. This is the point called the gate to the abyss, where the forces of the three mothers congregate. The many benefits of the purification of this point are clairaudiency and remembrance of lives past, although these memories do not come in a continuous succession of impressions.

The ceremonial emblem for this point is the knot of the head phylacteries that forms the letter 'D' (Daleth), and signifies the door. The streams of powers distributed from this point, going clockwise over the arms to create harmony are symbolized by the straps of the phylacteries hanging down to the waist.[20]

The ceremonial scarfs, tallith (prayer shawl), complex neckbands with symbols of life and death, fountains (or headless figures) that spray three streams of water, blood, and other fluids, long chains with intricate flower designs, skulls (or human heads) are emblems of this point.

The unification of the three upper points of knowledge, wisdom, and understanding, the highest goal of this work, will be completed at the end of the perfections when the door of perception on the larynx is opened.

The next step is the crossing of the abyss after which the exercises of "the way of the left" are abandoned. This is the time of St. George slaying the dragon (or the Leviathan, serpent, or basilisk), the sacrifice of Isaac, and the circumcision of Moses on the way to Egypt.

With this begins the third part of the work, the way of perfection emblematically shown as the middle pillar of the three of life, the entering of the Sanctum Sanctorum, or going into the temple by passing the two pillars and the three crosses on the Mount of Calvary.

THE THIRD EYE IN EGYPT, INDIA AND BALI

d. MERCY, RAḤAMIM

The names, numbers, and descriptions of the formative forces vary in different textbooks, for language is inadequate to describe what even experience cannot fully convey. The place of mercy is also called the one of compassion and clemency. By any name its place is in the area of the navel where a rib was taken from Adam to create Eve, our soul. By purification of this place we learn to communicate with all created things; the feelings of all creatures are perceived by this organ that holds harmony and health.

e. VICTORY, NEZAH

The point of Nezaḥ becomes active when the hands are laid just below the navel, an exercise that brings the strength necesary for the work of perfection.

f. FOUNDATION

This place of many names and functions harbors the foundation of life and for this reason is called the Yessod Ha-olam (foundation of the world). Powers from all over the body convene here to become part of the procreative forces.

The paramount importance assigned to this place becomes apparent by the study of the enormous amount of designs of serpents, dragons, vines, spiralling implements, the phallic sculptures, and meditative devices with designs of mandalas, yantras, and chacras.

The reversed triangle of mercy, victory, and foundation stands in opposition to the upright trinity of wisdom, knowledge, and understanding. When these powers unite in the heart, they form the shield of David.

38. The Serpent of the Paradise

> ...A king once had certain very precious stones which he kept locked away in a separate box in his palace. This king, in his wisdom, in order to keep prying eyes away from the casket took a dangerous serpent and wound it around the box thus effectually preventing anyone from stretching out his hand toward it...In likewise fashion the Holy One set about the inmost chamber of his presence a serpent of the "other side."
>
> Midrash Rabbah, Exodus 173: B

The actual purification begins with the awakening of the serpent-fire. Life energies well up from the feet to the sex organ, congregating there to flow through various channels to the head region.

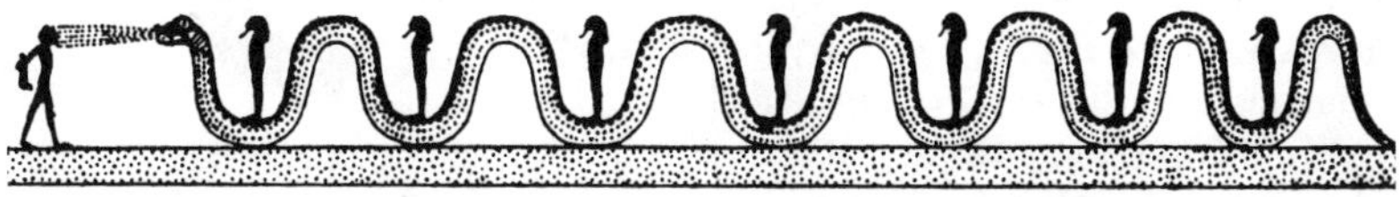

During this time we are confronted by an experience described in various phrases as "meeting the guardian of the treshold," encounter with the keeper of the world," or "angel with the flaming sword." These phrases signify that the students actually face their true selves. This encounter is also described as being examined by a mythical beast guarding the other world. The spinx, cerberus, custodian of the pylons or the devourer of the heart will obstruct the passage to the unworthy. The form of these animals is worth considering.

THE PATH OF THE RIGHT FIRE

The devourer of the heart for instance, has the head of a crocodile, the breast of a hyena, and lower parts of a hippopotamus or pig. In the Egyptian *Book of the Dead* this beast watches a scale on which the heart of man is weighed against the supreme truth. This means that, greed, fickleness, and desires stop progress and devour the impure heart.

The descriptions, terms, emblems, and works of art dealing with the "time of the serpent-fire" could easily fill a book. In spite of its allusions, comparatively little is known of the method of raising the fire *safely* and what to do when the guardian of the real self is encountered.

Again, art reveals what the scriptures conceal. The clearest symbol of the correctly activated serpent fire is the cadeceus. This staff of the healer Asclepius is identical with that of Hermes the herald of the Greek gods, who holds it in his *left* hand. On this emblem two serpents are entwined on a staff crowned with a winged globe, symbolizing the way.

Life energies should be activated clockwise, winding first from the right side, around the spine. The energy should pass through the sense-centers. The flow is reversed afterwards to the left side. When finally the spirit shoots up the spine, the work of purification is terminated.

At the end of the purifications, the fires must be subdued. This is dramatized by the tales of the heroes who slay dragons, serpents, basilisks, and various other fictitious beasts. The weapons of this fight indicate the termination of the purifications or the start of perfection.

In romances of the medieval knights slaying fabulous animals, they freed sleeping beauties, captive virgins, and queens all emblems of the soul.

Spirals as symbols for the serpent-fire, (i.e., the expanding bio-energies) are most commonly shown as winding staircases with three, five, or seven steps in (or outside) of towers; curved horns of rams; boar-fangs; serpents; and vines.

Terms and phrases for this "time of the serpent" are: going up the winding road, becoming captivated by vines, roses or thorny bushes, wounded by boars, overcome by flying serpents, or sacrifices of animals that were caught by their spiral horns in bushes or in trees of life.

The staff of Moses that turned into a serpent, serpents on crosses and trees, towers, pillars, pylons, scepters, and spears are emblems of the energies of the spine.

To rouse the serpent-fire safely the preparatory work must be completed. Solomon's Song of Songs (2:6), reveals: "...His left under my head, and his right embraces me...awaken not the love of higher spheres until it please..."[21]

The love of higher spheres is a profound secret of the "ATH" explained at the end of the book.[22]

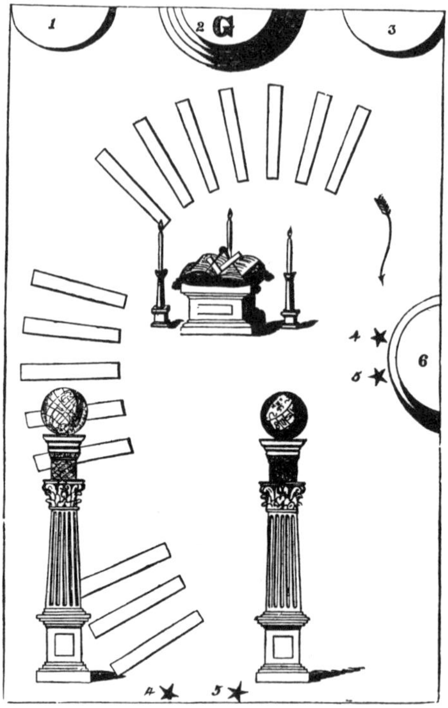

THE SPIRAL STAIRWAY OF THE MASON (1852)

Stances were the left hand is under the head and the right embraces the sex-organ are seen on many Egyptian Nordic and Indian works of art. Leaded glass windows and antique paintings show Adam and Eve in their flight from the garden; his left hand is behind his head to shield himself from the flaming sword of the angel; the right hand clutches fig leaves to cover his nakedness. The leaf of the fig tree resembles a hand, the fruit the vulva. Tradition has it that Adam and Eve partook of this fruit.[23] Others say that an apple got stuck in the throat of Adam. He turned blue just like Siva and other figures of myth and fairytales. Hence the significance of the fig and apple tree in the myths. The reason he turns a royal blue is told in another chapter.

The flames of the angel's sword spiral to the heavens. The sages said that its flames turn sometimes to the right and at other times to the left. Before their morning prayers, the orthodox Jews wind leather straps in seven spirals around the left arm. These, the phylacteries, represent ceremonially the serpent fire. A commentary to the Song of Songs remarks that the sages do not need the phylacteries. Day and night they wear them invisibly.[24] Spiral emblems resembling phylacteries are on Greek and Indian statues usually designed as serpents or vines.[25] [26]

The many references to vines, vineyards, and wine have an added significance. "Wine" is an emanation from God. Here is one tale:

Noah planted the vineyard, made wine, and got drunk in one day. By doing so right after leaving the ark, he sinned: He should have gone into his wife first. For this reason a lion castrated him and his seed was scattered. What does this tale mean? We have to be

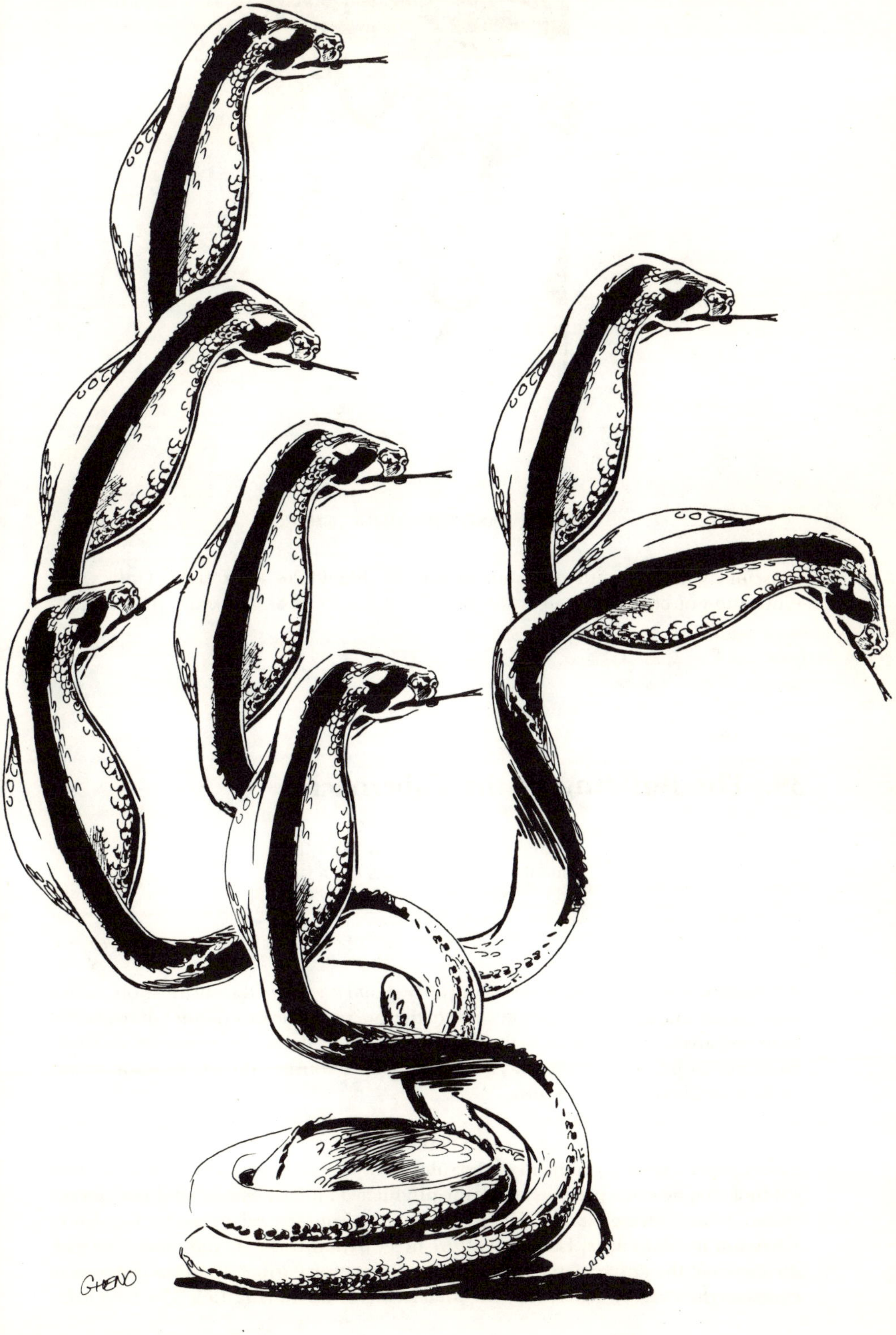
GHENO

ADAM AND EVE (GOTHIC CHURCH)

consciously united with our soul before the life forces are roused. Only when unification of body and soul is completed can the spirit of God enter into man.

39. The Building of the Tabernacle

> ...and the first beast was like a lion,
> and the second beast was like a calf,
> and the third beast had a face as a man,
> and the forth beast was like a flying eagle...
>
> Revelation 4:7

The numbers four, twelve, thirteen, and forty signal the end of the purification: At this time the initiate is led into the forecourt of the sanctum sanctorum, since the ways had been prepared for the coming of the master. The descriptions, commentaries about the building, the guarding of the tabernacle during the sojourn in the wilderness and their ciphers are linked to this grade.

a. CYPHER FOUR

The number four is an emblem of the subtle body for all stages of development from the time that he was a prisoner of the unenlightened until he enters "the house for the name of God" (King 1:8:20). The terms and emblems are: Adam (man), Garden of Eden and its four rivers, Israel as culture hero, nation, concept, and land. The four directions of the universe, the four mothers of the twelve tribes, the altar, and tent of meeting, the chariot, its wheels, the four living creatives (EZ. 1:5). The tabernacle

CREATING THE HIGHER SELF IN EGYPTIAN ART

(succah) and the four letters of the name of the Lord, Adonoi (A.D.N.I.) In its sequential sense the cypher stands for the body of initiations and the order of the themes during meditation.[27]

The medieval alchemist represented the four colors as: red and green lions, the black eagle or raven's head and the white king.[28]

b. CIPHER FORTY

The number forty stands for purifications with the letter M or W as symbol. This number is reached when the ten ineffable energies had been experienced on all four levels. Like a child that remains for forty weeks in the mothers' womb, so we remain for forty periods, days, weeks or years in the wilderness of our own nature. The materialistic nature is likened to water below. Two waters were created, one the celestial of the blessings, the other of the deep:

> ...God said, let there be a firmament in the midst of the waters and let it divide the waters from the waters...
>
> Gen. 1:6

This is why Moses, Elijah, Christ, and Buddha were resting above or beside the water at the hour of enlightment. They had reached a point beyond illusions.[29]

We would have to fast for forty days as they did and would have to be tempted as they were. Fasting is a code word of living in celibacy.

The terms water, rivers, springs, sea, etc. stand either for material things that destroyed the generation of the flood or for spiritual emanations from above. The predispersion root of the "water" and its glyphs are: M, W, V, N E S, ɬ, O

Root M or W: German — *w*asser
Russian — *v*ada
Hebrew — ***m***ayim
Japanese — ***m***isu
Swahili — ***m***ayi
Hungarian — *v*iz
.Finnish — *v*esi
Greek — ***n***autilo
Chinese — ***m***uing

c. CIPHERS TWELVE AND THIRTEEN

Who see those mighty ones
High in the heavens
Mighty in beauty?
Who sees the charioths
Holy and glorious?
Who sees the hosts in
The bright courts of glory
Exalting and praising
In awe and in fear
In joy and in wonder
The holy ones name?..
His thirteen paths of mercy
they gladly proclaim...

Zohar, III, Shemoth

The twelve simples are the basic functions in human beings, that, if not constantly, guided will obstruct the development of the higher self. By being purified they are transformed into guardians and aids on the way to perfection.

The number twelve is a code for either ruling or being ruled by food, sleep, sex, passion etc. To gain complete control over those twelve simple is the final work of the purification exercises. The unification of the physical emotional and intellectual powers can be achieved only after this is done. The actual unification is expressed by the cypher thirteen.[30]

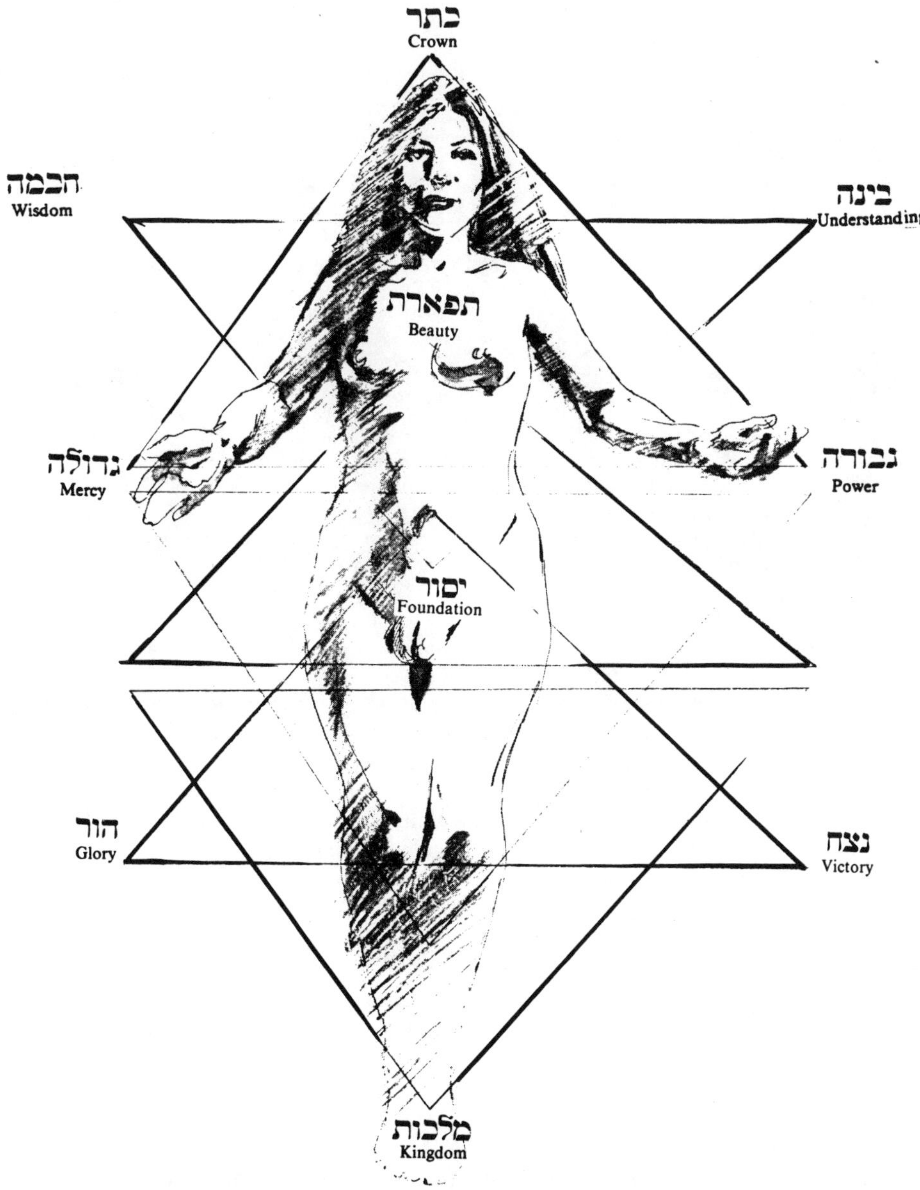

MACRO-ANTHROPOS

THE FIRST MAN, ADAM KADMON, FILLED THE UNIVERSE AND WAS GREATER THAN ALL THE ANGELS. *AD* = THE FIRST FORMING PRINCIPLE (MALE); *AM* = MATERIA PRIMA (FEMALE).

THE SIXTH KEY

> ...when he opened the sixth seal and, lo, there was a great earthquake; and the sun became *black*...
>
> Revelation 6:12

40. Elohim

> For so we have learned, that the *world to come* was created by ten (YOD=hand) and there wisdom remained hidden, the two being one. When God was crowned with ten crowns it was through the mystery of *the future world*, as already said. There was joy at this illumination, but all was in silence without a sound being heard.
> Wisdom then willed it to expand further, so that from that space there issued fire and water and air from which there sprang up a voice..."
>
> Midrash Rabbah Toldoth, 141 B

Following the purifications, the cloud (darkness, the black deeper than black) will guide you still further with the difference that you will see her now. On the gross level the attributes of the powers of Elohim came to us as in dreams; they appeared as the dark woman but now you will see their true nature, as the cloud that *led* Israel in the wilderness "*by day*" (Ex. 40:37) "...but if the cloud were not taken up, then they journeyed not till *the day* that it was taken up..." Note that the cloud led *by day* since the creation, because it was on the first day that, "there was darkness above the faces of the ABYSS and the powers of Elohim move over the faces..." (Gen. 1:1)

> ...By "darkness" I mean a lack of knowing, just as anything that you do not know or may have forgotten may be said to be "dark" to you, for you cannot see it with your inward eyes. For this reason it is called "a cloud" not of the sky, of course, but of unknowing and a cloud of unknowing between you and your God.
>
> "The cloud of unknowing" Walter Hilton 1300-49

The faces of the waters, a term for our gates of perception, now acquire knowledge and understanding of the powers of the Elohim. The veils that hide them are lifted up, one by one, until all seven are gone and we perceive, though still enigmatically, the manifestations of the formative forces. Through their actions, we experience (see, feel, and hear) supernal truth, love, faith, beauty, justice, and intelligence.

These are the intelligences (powers, vibrations, etc.) that form and reform the universe at his command; They lead us to the infinite center that channels the will of God to all created matter.

כתר
בינה
חכמה
פחד
חסד
רחמים
הוד
נצח
יסוד
מלכות

In the scriptures those forces are coded: the world created with ten words, the Torah that consists of ten words of the decalogue, the fingers of the hands as the chalice of benediction, ten crowns, ten degrees of wisdom, ten robes of God (Midrash Rabbah, Song of Songs IV:10) ten curtains of the Temple, ten pieces of silver, the goldspoon of ten shekels, the ten men that make a lawful assembly (minyan). All these allude to our innermost powers.[31]

From a few paragraphs about the force fields in the cabalistic Book of Formation, a vast literature developed attempting to explain the Sefirot. We find in these writings many contradictory attributes and symbols mixed with descriptive terms, attributes, and names of God not always cohesive as well as, names of angels, stars, directions of the universe etc.—all placed in terminologies that hides their true meaning.

What are the ten force fields? They are the essential bio-energies that cannot yet be explained. They move through our bodies with lightening speed. The rates and order-lines of their harmonious vibrations determine the state of our being, our health, mind, in short of our existence. The powers of the force fields come to the awareness through the gates of perceptions and channels that are for the initiate the *anatomy of higher self.*

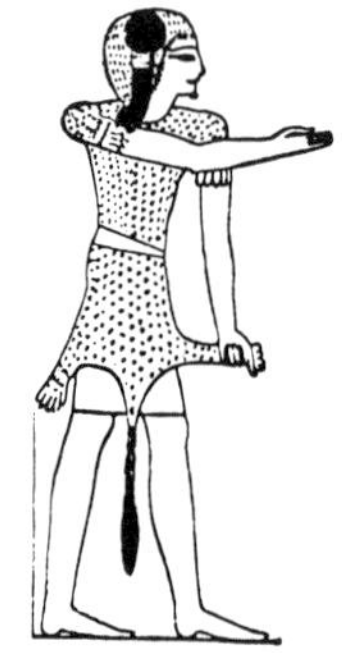
YOUNG EGYPTIAN INITIATE

The perfected, pure sensing points and the channels of their powers have as emblems the spots of blood, spotted pelts, bands, and stripes on garments, aprons, animals, and masks. Identical marks are on the thrones, chairs, the houses of initiates, and altars on which sacrifices are offered. The figures shown with these emblems are not necessarily priests or teachers, but quite possibly initiates, kings, or gods. By far the best representations of the anatomy of the self are the diagrams of the tree of life (and the cosmic tree, world tree, the cedars of Lebanon, a fig tree and an appeltree, a tamar (date palm), or the tree of death). The gates of perceptions are identical to those of the first man (androgyn) Adam Kadmon who had filled the universe and was greater than the angels. Dismembered giants and cultureheroes have the same significance, their parts being the building material of the universe. The figures of men covered with hundreds of symbols, serpents, flowers, and stars surrounded by designs of Gods and demons, as well as figures that are either fastened to or lie beneath a cross, a pillar, or a tree show the universal similarity of the concepts about the self.

In the tremendous variety of these designs, only a few main groups can be mentioned. The prostrate figures with demons, Gods, or dark gruesome women dancing, stepping, embracing or resting upon them. They are also symbolized by square and round designs filled with emblems and meaningful colors, the mandalas and yantras of the Hindu, Buddhists, and Lamaistic teachings with their different designs for each stage of the development are meditation accessories. This confusion makes personal supervision of the students' progress necessary.

All houses of worship are in one way or another emblems of our body, the temple "not build by hands" for during the raising of this temple "there was neither hammer nor ax nor any tool of iron heard." (I. King 6:7).

Symbols for the temple are holy mountains, staircases, ladders, ropes, vines and towers that reach the heavens, plus the odd pictures of the universe resting on a turtle or serpent.

The designs of the tree of life usually have three horizontal levels with their roots as the fourth representing *materia* (mother and soul).[33] This rather enigmatic emblem bridges the material and the spiritual worlds. The roots carry the pattern of the law of Elohim into all that had been formed. These spiritual patterns, while descending from the highest to the material levels, are clothed (veiled) seven times until their brightness

is dimmed sufficiently not to harm human beings with its splendor. What we know of the powers at first is their gross manifestations of fire, water, air, electricity, magnetism, light, and the twenty-two letters of the alphabet. This will be explained in the next chapter.

Each of the three levels has its own center. The lowest is the sex-organ, next comes the heart, and then the throat. These centers are the "ways and pillars" upon which the development of the self rests, the ways of the right, the left, and the way of equity, balancing fairness and justice.

The gates of perceptions on the tree are male and female but *the tree itself is Elohim who is female.*

> ...They said "up, make us a God," Ex II:1 Elohim, the Glory of Israel, she who rested upon them like a mother...
>
> KI-Tisa 191 a

When Elohim is comprehended in her reality and not through her attributes, the profile of supreme knowledge appears as "the little face" of the cabalist. The secret significance of the scriptures is revealed at that time. After this point the "simple terms" and stories will guide you further to hidden levels, called "SOD". SOD is the secret for which the scriptures use the terms, paradise (PRDS), garden of God, — of Eden, — of spices, — of cedars or fields, as in "...a closed garden is my sister and bride..." (Song of Songs 4:12).

Of the many code words used to describe each of the forcefields, love, beauty, wisdom, justice, understanding, strength, majesty, continuity of life, knowledge, and creativity come closest suggesting to their nature, although no expressions can describe their true nature. The sages found it wise to call the forcefields Belih-mah, the ineffable, because their powers are far too overwhelming to be understood.

To approach them, each one of the "names of the Lord" has to vibrate in *each* of the gates of perception. Coded in emblematic form, ten concentric circles, stars, points signs, or letters are assigned to each point of the tree. This is very important.

41. The Ten Force-Fields

The forcefields are: (1) the continuity of life, roots, the kingdom (really "the queendom"), materia, and soul with the name *Malkhut;* (2) the creativity in the center of the first level (the first court of the temple) called *Yesod Ha-Olam,* the foundation of the world from which the three procreative forces issue. The other two points on this level are (3) the majesty of life, *Hod,* and (4) the strength, *Nezah.* These three points of perception form the spiritual pattern of the world and are the support of the work of perfection.

(5) The beauty of life, *Tiferet,* in the center of the second level (second court) keeps the balance between the fearful power of (6) divine justice, *Din,* and (7) divine love, *Hesed.* The level is the first source of inner light.

The guiding principels of life are on the third level (the third court) called (10) the crown, *Keter,* or faith, *Daat,* as the center of supreme knowledge. Bound to the crown are (8) understanding, *Binah,* and (9) divine wisdom, *Hohma.*[34]

a. COLORS

The colors that appear during these meditations will show you the most active sensing points at this moment. The intensity and purity of their color indicates how far you have advanced. The color of Daath is a golden flecked white that will turn brilliant white at the end of the purification, "to become seven times brighter than the sun, while the moon (wisdom) will shine like the sun." Malkuth is first black, and will turn to gold at the end; all other colors are muddy before the purifications.

When all the colors appear at once in their brightest hues, you will be in possession of the robe of many colors and ready for the next level of work.

In order to *accelerate the work of perfection,* project the correct color into the least active gate of perception.[34] [35]

b. THE LAW

The forcefields teach us in wonderful ways how to live a perfect life in beauty, love, justice, greatness, strength, wisdom, knowledge, understanding, and majesty. *This is the substance of what religion teaches* and not more.

Meditating upon these precepts, you will be led to new spiritual heights. Conforming with the law, the Sheḥina remains in her rightful place, and the spiritual sabbath can be celebrated.

This day we rest from the work of perfection. We welcome this day with a dance before the Lord, stamping three times with the right and three times with the left foot.

THE SEVENTH KEY

> ...and when he had opened the seventh seal,
> there was silence in heaven
> about the space of half an hour
> and I saw the seven angels
> which stood before God; and to them were given seven trumpets..."
>
> Revelation 8:1-2

42. The Twenty-Two Buildingstones

The Hebrew alphabet has twenty-two letters and each one is an emblem of supernal harmonies. They are the attributes of the creative, "Shem", the word of God. The Talmud speaks of sages who had reached such spirituality that they could create when reciting the word.

The vibrations of the word form the formless in the universe and in the self of man. This is symbolyzed in the work of perfection where the twenty-two vibrations are experienced as the three mothers, seven doubles, and the twelve singles.

> ...the formless He formed and from the non-existent existence came. And He carved a great column out of intangible spirit. Here is the evidence: Observe, exchange (letters) and make all that has to be made on the highest level (Ath-)till all words become one name of God. And the evidence of this matter: the twenty-two forces in one body...
>
> Book of Formation .2:6

The words of power had been given for the purification and perfection of the self, but now, the words are no longer spoken; they are energies that as sounds of music, forms, and dances flow in geometric patterns with, in, and around the body. At this time the true word is revealed. Its powers circulate around and through the body in spirals, pentagrams, triangles, and figures that resemble the movements of the primary electrons we see in a bubble-chamber. And just as we learned in the beginning to project the powers of the enlivened hands in the figure of the pentacle around us so do we now take the lights of our body in the hands and weave them around in figures of eight. We wrap beams of the silver light of Sheḥinah in spirals around us and let the golden light of the Elohim protect us.

This is the secret of the force called Malkuth, roots, sister, bride, mother, queen and Shehinah who is the "Ath" of the Bible. This term consists of the first and last letter of the alphabet and cannot be translated. Its meaning goes far beyond words, encompassing the whole of creation (from A-Z, the alpha and omega). Written before the name of Sarah, she is no longer the legendary wife of the patriarch but ruler of the soul: Ath-Sar-H is an attribute of all forces of the soul.

In the very first sentence of Genesis 1:1, the word "Ath" appears twice, "...Bereshit Bara Elohim *Ath* Ha-Shamayim-Ve-*Ath* Ha-Aretz..." "...In the beginning God created..." He created these five: the Elohim, ath, heavens, ve-ath-earth. The first all encompassing force is expressed by the word "ath" as the Sheḥinah that stands between the Elohim and the heavens. The second "ath" links the heavens and the earth and has a prefix the letter Vav (VE) to teach that 'V', the bio-energy, is its leading power. But can our soul become a bridge between the heavens and the forcefields?

No, she cannot by herself, the Sheḥinah, our soul will not rise up but Elohim will draw her up to be united with her. The unification of the soul and Elohim, i.e., ten forcefields and the supernal twenty-two letters are the thirty-two ways of wisdom. The number thirty-two is written L=30; B=2 & L b—meaning the heart, the meeting, and mating place of God. 'L' signifies the center, *l*eader, *l*earning. 'B' is the temple, *B*eit-ha-kodesh, *b*lessing, *b*raha. At this time, the heart becomes the center of learning, the holy of holies in which the law and the blessing of God rest.

We have learned that the Shehinah surrounds the body, as the leaves of a flower enclose and hold the pistil. So do the forces of the soul protect us while the supernal faith sends its light into the self and from this union, the higher self emerges. Philo Judaeus has said that the creation of the world could be compared to intercourse. And: "...when a man puts his arms around his wife, and she is close to him, nothing more has to be said..."

This is the end of the initiation into the lower level of the Cabalah.

COMMENTARIES AND EXTRACTS

1. The ten force-fields are intermediaries between God and the Universe. As symbols they are a point in the center of a circle, or the letter "i" in the Hebrew script. Each one of the letters of the hebrew and sanscrit alphabeth represent one formative energy emanating from the forcefilds. To show this, all Hebrew letters are formed from this one letter "i". In Sanscrit all letters are bound by a line hovering between the upper and the lower level of the script. The symbolic meaning is obvious.

As a symbol the hebrew letter ="I" with the numerical value ten stands for spirit of God and the supernal fire. As the first letter of the hidden name of God, the design shows how the right point receives power from above to dispense energies through the left point to the world.

This is to teach you to give of what you received from above; not wealth, happiness or knowledge but yourself.

The symbol of the force-fields in action is in all religions a point moving.

2. Three Mothers:

> "In the universe (space) AIR, WATER and FIRE. The heavens were in the beginning produced from fire, the earth from water and the wind from the air, which thus balances the two."
>
> Three Mothers:
>
> "In the year (Time)=the cold, the heat and the temperate state. The heat came from the fire, the cold from the water and the temperate state from air, balancing the two."
>
> Three Mothers:
>
> "In man=the head, the belly and the chest. The head comes from the fire, the belly from the water and the chest from the air, balancing the two."
>
> Sefer Yezirah, III, 5-7

3. "...Abram and Abraham are the same...Isaac too was called Abraham and Abraham was called Israel. Isaac was called Israel and Jacob was called Israel..."

> Midrash Rabah, Toledoth 53:5

That these forces are also: knowledge, understanding and wisdom, is explained in Zohar Pekudei 3:bl:

> "...fire is knowledge (superior perception). Water is understanding air is wisdom..."
>
> Therefore it is said in the proverbs XXIV 4-5:
>
> "...with wisdom is the house built and by understanding it is established and by knowledge shall the chambers be built..."

The number three in the human being is the: mind and fire=the head; lust and water=the belly; while the air, the heart hold mind and lust in balance.

On the head: the brain is the fire; the mouth is the water; and the nose, ears, and eyes as the center of the sense organs direct and keep balance between the brain and the mouth.

In the brain the three are: the back of the head=the water; the forehead=the fire; the crown=the air that balances both.

4. The trinity of the soul comes in three consecutive steps to the awareness during initiations. The vital principals awake first in the Nefesh (water) then in the spiritual vehicle of the Ruaḥ (air) and are unified in Neshama (fire) the real soul.

"...observe that NEFESH, RUAḤ and NESHAMAH are on ascending series of grades. The lowest of them, NEFESH, has it sources with the help of RUAḤ, which abides between Fire and Water. *RUAḤ IN ITS TURN IS SUSTAINED BY NESHAMAH* that higher grade above it, which is thus the source of both NEFESH and RUAḤ. When Ruaḥ receives its sustenance from Neshamah, the Nefesh receives it in turn through Ruaḥ, so that the three form a unity."

Zohar, II, 206A

5. The Rabbis said, that the word "that created the world" will maintain the wise and destroy the foolish.

> "...By the word of the Lord were the heavens made, and all the host of them by the breath of the mouth (PS. XXXIII:6): Not by labor or toil but only by a word: thus, *"AND GOD SAID: LET THERE BE LIGHT"* (YEHIEH OR) (by these two means created he, by *word* and by *breath*)..."
>
> Midrash Rabbah, III:2

The word Yehieh (let there be) is written in the secret of the great name that Moses received in the flames of the thorn bush and is translated properly 'I shall be'. The phrase Yehieh Or is therefore understood: 'I will be your light' as the promise of the coming of the supernal light. How the word creates has been explained, how the breath creates we learn. The word breath (RUAḤ) can be translated as air, wind, breath of life and spirit of God and we will experience the RUAḤ of God on these four levels.

The words of power given in this book for the preparatoy work are from the Zohar: they are "M-I-H" for the fire exercises, "M-A-H" for the air "H-O-U" for the water sign and used all through the first exercises. Two names of God have to be contemplated at the same time (but not spoken) because "a prayer that is spoken is not heard". The most mysterious attribute is *never prounounced* but written IHVH: The Christians transcribed this name Jehovah and the Greeks Jahveh. The gnostics used an incredible amount of variations of this name such as: IOA, IAO, AEEH, HHIIIO, OOOYYYY, YYOO, YOIYHIYHIYHIXI, etc. (Budge, Egyptian magic). The priests of Mandaeans, the Nasoraeans (priests from the Academy of Nazareth) used the names IAOAR, SIOS, SHIBA, YAUUA, etc. All that shows that the pronounciation of the Great Name was not divulged. And for good reasons.

In Chapter 1, Mishna 16 of the Book of Formation this name, the Shem-ha-mephorash is elucidated: "the IHVH becomes a name of three vowels, with six possible combinations of the name:

OAI AOI
OIA IOA
AIO IAO

Each one of these combinations is used for a different exercise. Other combinations are:

*A*BR*A*H*A*M—AAA
*I*S*A*AC—IAA
*J*ACOB—*IAO*

for the three levels of intiations.

Endless variations of the ineffable name of God exist: TIO, DIAO, DAO, DEUS, DIUS-FIDIUS, DIONYSUS, ZIO, DEIVO, DIOS, THEUS, ZEUS.

One of the great attributes of God is called "Adonoi." The "Ad" stands for the air, 'on' for water and 'o-i' for fire. Rabbi Abraham B. Isaac said that the word is read "Lord of the o-i", Adon-o-i, the ruler of the world.

6. Phrases for the two numbers are: the forty nine gates of understanding, the forty nine windows to the heavens through which we see the stars (awakened organs), 50 gates of the Jubilee year, Binah (understanding) that opens the fifty gates, (Binah=force field of celestial waters, female). The forty nine aspects of the Torah are remembered by the number of days between Passover and Pentecost (this symbol goes very deep) and the 50th day, celebrated for the mystery of the Torah.

The numbers are also indicative of the tremendous mystery of the charioth the greatest of all secrets of the ten force fields.

In the Bible spiritual sense organs are mentioned in the Song of Songs: "...I am the *Rose of Sharon and the Lily of the Valleys...*" Seals (S.S. VIII) "...Place me like a seal upon thy hearrt, like a seal upon thine arm. Its coals are coals of fire, a very flame of the Lord..."

The dormant, not yet purified organs, are "the faces of the waters" (Gen. 1/2) the pane'i ha majim. On the highest level, they are the princes of the heavenly faces, the 'Malhei Panim' and the faces of the shabbath 'Pnei Sabbath'. The S.S.O.s are further: flowers, candles, doors of perceptions, gates of conception, kings, speckled dress of the initiate, Nekudoth=points (Tree of Life, Luria-Vital), lights, lamps and Kelim (the tools). They are the spotted, striped, and ringed animals of Jacob and the striped, blood spotted and ringed skins and aprons worn by high priests and intiated nobelmen. The spots are the emblems for the active points of perceptions while the stripes are the connecting channels. As feline symbols they are the striped or spotted panther in the Congo, tiger in India and China, cat in Egypt and jaguar and ocelot in the Americas. Further: the cups of benediction, lightened faces, cherubs, wheels, cauldrons and the feathers of headgears of the American indians. They are the Roses of the Sufis and lotus flowers in India, China, Japan and Egypt.

7. Here is a Cabalistic description and the terms for the Gates of perception.

> "...(The spiritual body) is called 'hall of the Tabernacle'. There all those windows are to be found, on this side and on that, and it holds all the arrangements of the Tabernacle. Six of the windows are greater than all the others and one, which is concealed, rules over them. One of these seven is called 'the window of light' and into it the star, which the wise call Yad (hand) enters... when that star comes out, it stretches out a hand with five rays, which are five fingers, which shine and sparkle in that window'..." (The S.S.O. Spinalcenter near the navel, on the Tree of Life, represented by strength.)
>
> "...The second window is called 'the window of the claw' because it has the form of a claw...it is known to the wise as 'viper'..." (the S.S.O. of the left side of the Tree of Life: justice.)

"...The third window is called 'Breastplate'. A star enters into it, called 'Bright Light'...peace, satisfaction and harmony prevail throughout the world..." (The S.S.O. of the heart, on the Tree of Life: beauty.)

"...The fourth window is called 'Challice' and the star which enters into it is called by the wise 'Cluster of Cypress flowers' because it comes out like a cluster and spreads it rays in the form of grapes...much procreation takes place in the world at this time..." (The S.S.O. of the Phallic Region, named foundation on the tree; Do not read 'GRAPES' but 'VINES'; its rays encircling the body like vines.)

"...The fifth window is called 'Cistern' because the star which enters it always 'draws' like a bucket and is never at rest; the wise of heart can never discover its real nature since it never remains still. They therefore, only with great difficulties examine it and come to some conclusion about it..."(The S.S.O. of the throat, the wisdom of the Tree.)

"...The sixth window is called 'Brightness' and a star enters into it called Gazron, because when it reigns over the world it is a sign of judgment...the reign of the heathen nations will be terminated and Israel shall rule over them and there will be fulfillment of the words 'moreover the light of the moon shall be as the light of the sun (Isa. XXX 26)..." (The S.S.O. on the forehead, the place of the head tefilin on the Tree of Life the Sphere of understanding.)

"...and then will this cause the seventh window to open to the whole world whose star is the 'Star of Jacob'...top of head..." (The S.S.O. on top of the head, the crown of the Tree of Life.)

Zohar, Terumah Exodus 172a

Term: Star of David=Heart; seal of the third level of initiation
Term: Jacob =Initiate on the way to wisdom
Term: Israel =The perfect being

8. The enormous importance of the work on the seven doubles is shown by the great amount of terms and symbols used for them in all the ancient scriptures.

"...Their foundations
he engraved them
he formed them
he purified them
he weighed and combined them
and formed seven stars, seven days of the year
and seven gates on the body
and from them he engraved seven heavens,
seven earths and seven sabbaths.
Therefore: He loved the seven under all the heavens..."
Book of Formation IV. Mishnah 6: seven doubles expressed by the letters B, G, D, K, P, R, TH

The references and aspects of the sacred number seven are far too numerous to be possibly explored in this study. The cabalistic works point repeatedly to the number seven as having only one significance.

"...The number seven has everywhere a similar symbolism, e.g. the seven maidens and the seven chamberlains mentioned in the Book of Esther (Esther II, 9:1, 10) R. Isaac said (in the commentary to 'Joseph in Egypt') that the seven good kine symbolize the superior grades and the seven lean and ill-favoured kine other and lower grades; the former of the side of holiness, and the latter of the side of

> defilement. SEVEN EARS OF CORN, R. Judah said: 'the first seven ears were good, as they came from the right side, of which it is written 'that it was good' (Gen. 1, 4) and the second seven were ill, as being lower as the others; the first one proceeded from the side of purity, and the others from the side of impurity..."
>
> Zohar. II:194 A

The phrase 'the right and left way' has already been explained. However, the above quotation uses the phrase differently and poses the question: why are the good terms mentioned first and the bad ones next? What are the right and left ways?

> "...and his right hand is a fiery law fo them;
> That is the TORAH.
> and his left hand is his Power;
> These are the Tefilin..."
>
> Talmud. Berahot. bl: 6a

Note: *we are free to enter the way of the right hand. But once we enter the way of the left, the way of the serpent, we cannot turn back any more and have to obey the law.*

9 Example of Cabalistic Gematria
The supernal powers of Elohim (the ten sefirot) have the letter (i) as emblem with a numerical value of ten. The letter "i" was taken from Sarai's name (mother of Isaac) and replaced by the letter "h". Sara-i as written in hebrew) meaning "ruled by God" becomes Sar-h (as written in Hebrew) "ruled by the soul". Since "h" has the numerical value of five, the "h" of the ten forces was given to Abram (father of faith) and he becomes Abraham, the "father of highest mercy." Abraham and Sarah, when perfected are fruitful in their union.

> "...he said to Abraham in effect; (Shabbath 156-b) give up they astrological speculations; this is not the way to aquire a knowledge of my name. Thou seest, but I see also. ABRAM, it is true, is not to beget children, but ABRAHAM will beget children...."
>
> Zohar. V, Naso 148A

To clarify: The force fields "i"=10 are divided into upper and lower "h"=5. The upper field is mercy and the lower is justice and their union created Isaac (mirth). This is one of the many secrets of the Holy Name I*HVH*.

This secret was explored in the last chapter, concerning the two 'ath' of the creation, whose numbers can be read either 401 or 5.

> "...as the shabbat is rest for all, so the shabbatical year is rest for the spirit and the body. Observe that the 'H' (in God's name) denotes rest for higher and lower — the higher 'H' for the higher and the lower for the lower. The higher 'h' is seven years only; the one is a sabbatical year the other a Jubilee; and when closely scrutinized *both are found to be one...*"
>
> Zohar. V, Behar, Leviticus, 108a/2

10. More details about the seven doubles are in the chymical wedding of the alchemists in the story of the birth of Isaac after the coming of three angels and in all "immaculate conceptions".

> "...And she conceived and bore Cain (Gen. IV,1) R. Eleazar B. Azarian said: 'Three wonders were performed on that day: On that day they were created (Adam and Eve), on that very day they cohabited, and on that very day they produced offspring'. R. Joshua B. Karhah said 'only two entered the bed, and seven left it: Cain and his twin sister, Abel and his two twin sisters..."
>
> Midrash Rabbah

11. In the Bible the renouncing of the low desires before the start of purifications are tales of violence: 'the first born children of the Egyptians are slain, the Pharao and his host are drowned as was the generation of the flood'. So are also the counterattacks of all desires that hamper the spiritual development portrayed as violent acts: the attempt of the Pharaoh to drown the first born Jewish children or the killing of the babes in Beth-leḥem.

For us, these tales and the regulations for sacrifices, are allusions to the spiritual developments and commentators wrote quite openly about this deeper significance.

Example of self-sacrifices:

> "...But we are poor and have not the wherewithal to bring sacrifices. God replied: I desire words, as it says; take with you words, and return into the Lord and I will pardon your sins..."
>
> Midrash Rabbah, Exodus XXXVIII,4

12. "...Rabbi Abin said in Rabbi Simeon' name: God assisted Abraham with his *right* hand to circumcise him, as it says: 'Thou madst the circumcision with him' (NEH IX:8)..."

> Middrash Rabbah, Song of Songs, V:1

Other concealed covenants were made with Noah, Isaac, Jacob, Moses, and David.

> "...Israel (the initiate) is linked to God, and by what? By the holy impress on their flesh. We have learnt that the Torah is called covenant, and God is called 'covenant' and this impress is called 'covenant' and so all is inseparable linked together..."
>
> S.V. Ahare Moth 73b

Once the spiritual circumcision is understood, the commentaries make sense. Here is an example from the commentaries about Jacob and the ladder:

> "...and he was afraid, and said: How full of awe is this place...it refers to the mark of the Holy Covenant, which should not be left inoperative...Jacob then said: This is none other than the House of God, implying: This is not to remain idle. Its covenant is not meant to exist in isolation...it is in sooth a Godly abode, to be used for the promotion of fecundity and for receiving blessings from all the bodily organs. For indeed this is the Gate of *Heaven*. Or in other words, the Gate of the body; the Gate assuredly..."
>
> Zohar, IV, Vaiereh 150b

13. Another instant: The word grass stands for "life of man".

> "...In the morning they are like grass which groweth up.
> in the morning it flourishes and groweth up;
> in the evening it is cut down..."
>
> Ps. 90:5-6

For the Cabalists the term connotates the spiritual life energies.

> "...R. Hiya expounded the verse: 'He causeth grass to grow for the cattle' (Ps. CIV,14) 'The grass', he said 'refers to the sixty thousand myriads of angels who were created on the second day of creation, being all of flaming fire; and they are called 'Grass' because they are constantly cut down and restored. They are food for 'catttle' over which rules 'man'..."
>
> Zohar, II/15

'cattle'=term for multitude, 'man'=term for the leader, the initiate.
The feeding of multitudes on the Sea of Galilea is understood thus: *the multitude had spiritual food from 5 barley loaves*

> "...make the men sit down. Now there was *much grass* in the place, so the men sat down, in number *five thousand*..."
>
> St. Mark 8/21 and St. John 6/10
>
> "...gathered them together and filled *12* baskets with the fragments of the barley loaves..."
>
> 6/13
>
> "...when I broke 5 loaves among *five* thousand, how many baskets full of fragments took ye up? They say unto him TWELVE..."
> "...and when *seven* among *four* thousands, how many basekts full of fragments took ye up? And they said, *SEVEN*..."
> "...And He said unto them: How is it that ye do not understand?..."
>
> St. Mark 8/19

14. "...It was God who wedded to Moses the Ethiopian woman, who stands for 'resolve' unalterable, intense, and fixed' For this Moses merits praise, that he took the Ethiopian woman, i.e., the nature that has been tried by fire and cannot be changed. For, even as in the eyes, the part that sees is black, so the soul's power of vision has the title of 'woman of Ethiopia'..."

Philo, Allegoriate Interpretation 1167-69

The next quotation illustrates how, by the use of various terminologies, the start of the initiation is presented. Frame of the narrative: Rabbis going *the way* and discussing the Torah.

> "...R. Eleazar discoursed on the verse: "O Lord, in the morning shalt thou hear my voice..." etc. (ps. V,4) "When daylight comes he said, that "morning" of Abraham awakes (the begin of spiritual vision) and then is a time of grace for all, both virtuous and wicked, and therefore it is the hour to offer prayer to the Holy King..." "...in the morning will I order my prayers into thee and keep watch..." Why is the word MORNING repeated? One refers to the morning of Abraham (the first level of work) and the second to the morning of Joseph (the last level)..."
> "...the first light that God created was so bright that the world could not endure it. God therefore made another light as vestment to this one, and so with all the other lights, until all the worlds could endure the light without being dissolved. Hence grades were evolved and lights were wrapped in each another until they reached this "morning of Joseph" *WHICH WAS A SUBSTRATUM TO ALL the higher lights*___"
>
> *Zohar. Balak 204a-204b*

This paragraph closes with the keys to the passage:

> "...As the rabbis were going along a pigeon approached..." "...As they went along a raven came and stood before them croaking loudly..."
>
> Zohar. Balak 204a-204b

15. "Thus we have learned that the Torah was written with black fire on white fire" (Zohar). This part is explained in depth by Zohar. V, Balak.

> "...I am black but comely, O Ye daughters of Jerusalem (S.S. 1.5) "This means that when she (The Kalah, the low seal of Malkuth) is very lovesick for her beloved, she shrinks to nothing until only a dot is left of her and she is hidden from her hosts (spiritual sense organs) and camps.Then she says "I am black, like the letter

Yod. . ." (= # 10 - symbol for the ten force fields, the first emanation of God at the creation, also ELOHIM) in which there is no white space, and I have no room to shelter you under my wings; therefore "do not look at me", *FOR YOU CANNOT SEE ME AT ALL.*" What then do her mighty warriors do? (the active S.S.O) They roar like lions (the first wheel of the chariot, the awakening of the serpent fire) until their voice is heard by the beloved above, and he knows that his beloved is love-sick like himself, so that none of her beauty can be seen and so through the voices of those warriors of hers, her beloved comes forth from his palace with many gifts and presents, with spices and incense, and comes to her and finds her black and shrunken, without form or beauty. He then draws near to her and embraces and kisses her until she gradually revives from the scents and spices. . ."

16. ". . .Some are gifted with a supersoul "NESHAMAH" some with the impulse of the spirit "RUAḤ" and some only with an ordinary soul "NEFESH". Those who attain no higher than the ordinary soul, cling to the side of uncleanliness, and when they sleep, unclean things come and cling to them and show them things in dreams, partly true and partly false. Hence heathens also see true things sometimes in their dreams. Now those evil species are of three grades. The highest are suspended in the air, the lowest mock men in their dreams. The intermediate grade tell men things partly true and partly false, but if true, only relating to the immediate future. As for the higher grade for those who are suspended in the air, when the soul NEFESH of a man seeks to prepare itself for the reception of the spirit RUAḤ, something issues from it and seeks to rise and in so doing meets those spirits which tells it things that will happen, both in the near and in the more distant future."

17. ". . .and it draws to that grade until it acquires spirit. When it has done so, the spirit issues forth and cleaves its way through rocks and mountains, until it ascends among the holy angels and there it learns many things before returning to its place. This is as far as a man can attain holiness, until he is endowed with a supersoul NESHAMAH. . ."
Zohar. IV VAYIKRAH, 25a

18. ". . .the spirit of the Lord *began* to *ring* in Samson, it. . .(began in three places). . .(1) and behold a young lion *roared* against him. And the spirit of the Lord came mightily upon him. . .(2) and after a while he *returned* to take her (carcass of the lion). . .(3) and behold there was a *swarm of bees* in the body of the lion, and honey, and he scraped it out into his hands and *went on, eating as he went.*"

The sound perceptions of the roar of the lion signals the arousing serpent or as expressed in the Zohar: "the intertwined mysteries" begin.

". . .Putting his hands crosswise (Gen. XLVII/20) . . .that is, he first raised up his right hand. . .he then saw that the Shehinah (soul) is in the west (throat, head). The reason for this as has been explained, is that she may be between north and south (heart) in an attitude of nuptial union, with the north (left hand) supporting her beneath her head and the south (right hand) embracing her (the sex-organ). So says the Scripture: "let his left hand be under my head, and his right hand embrace me. . ." "The following is a mystery known to those, who inhabit the south and has been sent to us by our "breathren who arrange the lamps". That you may effect unification by means of the intertwined mysteries (serpent) that are of the shape of the celestial intertwining, accept upon yourselves the first thing every day the yoke of the Holy Kingdom; thereby will you enter into the Holy intertwining of the south. These encircle the sides of the world (the spiritual body) until they become bound up in one knot "*but keep firm hold of the south*" and there abide. . ."

The right hand must stay in command all through this part of the work. By directing the powers to flow in controllable pattern from the right to the left in and around the body, they purify, heal, and nourish the body. These powers converge in centers flow through channels that become alive and vibrant for a time. When the right hand strokes the body, overly strong vibrations will subside. When the palms are held up you receive; facing down, the hands will give and forming a fist you hold the blessings and forces in yourself.

All the exercises conclude with the sign of the circumcision, moving the right hand swiftly across the body:

> "...from Rabbi Simeon...have we heard in exposition...the flowing most recondite doctrine: As long as the foreskin rest upon the sign of the holy covenant, the holy principle is prevented from disclosing the mystery of the covenantal sign. But when the bright light enters therein and separates between foreskin and holiness, the result is HASHMAL (Hash=speedy; Mal=circumsion) to which there is a speedy uncovering of circumcision..."
>
> Zohar. IV, 203b

Term: Hashmal (electricity)=the appearance of sefirothic powers.

19. The organ of the crown, the final step on the way to perfection, has the last letter of the Hebrew alphabet 'th' as emblem. As the last letter in a word, the 'th' is understood cabalistically as the termination of the physical, emotional, and intellectual achievements. We read therefore: tru*th*=eme*th* as the teachings of the Torah. Emeth, written Amth is a word of many meanings and changes to dea*th* when the 'A' is taken away. 'A' stands for God and the saying goes that Amth (emeth— without 'A' is 'Mth': "Truth without God is death."

The letter combination of Mth is read: M=illusion; Th=end; death is the end of illusion.

The root of death, 'Mth', is found in many languages, indicating that this root came from the generation before the dispersion — Moerder (German) — Mata (Indonesian) — Mort (French) — Metall (Mayan) — Mat (Arabic) — Smrt (Serbian) — Muerte (Spanish) — Mortalis (Latin).

20. To enliven this point we place the right hand under the head in the sign of the 'A' which resembles the 'Daleth' of the Hebrew alphabet: "...Your left hand embraces me..." (S.S.)

21. "...what is meant by "Thou shalt see my back? (Ex. XXXIII, 23) which as we have learned, means the knot of the Phylacteries. "so we have explained and this is the truth of the matter and therefore a strap hangs down below to show that *all below are sustained by this,* and therefore a sign upon they hand..."

22. How are the powers of the fire released?

> "...His left hand is under the head and his right hand embraces me..."
>
> Song of Songs 11/6 and VIII/3

This passage is followed by a warning, appearing three times in the "Song of Songs":

"...I adjure you, Daughters of Jerusalem
by the Gazelles (Be-Zebaoth) and by the
Hinds of the field That you awaken not,
Nor stir up love
Until it pleases...--

II/7

The power is love and the right hand embraces the place where the fire rests. The vibrations of the word Zebaoth (the Lord of hosts) is the sound of this power.

This is further explained: "...His left hand..." This refers to the phylacteries (of the left arm) emblematic for the fire that goes from right to left, just as the right hand winds the throngs over the left arm.

"...The left hand under the head..." is the first table of the commandments and the right hand the second table. Both tables, the broken and the whole one, *rest in the Ark of the covenant.*

The ark of the covenant of Moses and Noah, the missing stone of the arc, the casket of the Eucharist (Arca), Arcanum magnum, etc., as well as the description and measurements of the different arks, refer to the point of the foundation. Arche=beginning (Greek).

"...Make thee an ark (VI, 14)...The meaning of make thee a fiery serpent" (Numb. XXI, 8) is not clear. (since, Moses was not told how) R. Judah said in R. Assis name: The wise man may hear, and increase in learning (Prov. 16) applies to Moses, who reasoned thus: "if I make it of gold or of silver these words do not correspond to the other. Hence I will make it of Brass (Neḥosheth), since this word corresponds to the other Na-*Ḥash*=serpent (Ne-*Ḥosh*-Eth brass).

This refers to the middle pillar on the tree of life made from brass with the right pillar from the gold of the sun and the left one the silver of the moon.

The word Na=Ḥash means serpent; the word for brass is Na-Ḥosh-Eth; and speedy circumcision is Ḥash-Mal.

The root, Ḥash, in all those words is read cabalistically:

— Ḥ=protected enclosure (of)
— Ȧ=the first
— Sh=fire

By this we are given to understand that the foundation of the middle pillar is the protected enclosure of the first fire. Mark this well.

23. "...and the serpent said to the woman (the soul) ye shall not surely die: 5)"...for God doeth know that in the day ye eat thereof your eyes shall be opened, and ye shall be as God, knowing good and evil..."

Gen. 3/4/5

And they ate and their eyes were opened and they saw each other as they really were, the man saw his soul and the soul the real man, and both were ashamed.

"The eyes of them both were opened."

Midrash Gen. XIX/6

"...were they then blind?...He showed them how many generations they had destroyed..."

Midrash Gen. III/7

We see how much we have destroyed through ignorance when our eyes are opened. "...and then they heard the voice of the Lord travelling." Note: It is the voice that is travelling, the voice of the Lord "a fire, leaping and ascending."

According to Midrash Gen. XIX/4: "Only the woman *saw* the words of the serpent" because it is only the soul that has the visions of higher realms.

> "...and the woman said to the serpent: "of the fruit of the Trees of the garden we may eat. (III,2) 'Now where was Adam during this conversation? Abba Halfon ben Korian said: "he had engaged in intercourse and then fallen asleep" Rabbi Joshua ben Karman: "Because he (the serpent) saw them engaged in their natural function and conceived a passion for her." The rabbi said: "God took Adam all around the world...through a land that no man passed through and where no man dwelt. (Jer. II/6)..."
>
> Midrash Rabbah XIX, 3/4

> "...but because he had eaten of its fruit, the figtree opened its door and received him..."

> "...Of what species was the figtree? R. Abin said it was Berath Sheba..."
>
> Midrash Rabbah 12:7

(Berath Sheba—creator of seven or the source of seven) i.e., the word figtree stands for the higher body.

> "...And the Lord send fiery serpents..." This accords with the text: "...Who so breaketh through a fence, a serpent shall bite him..."
>
> (Eccl. X, 8)

When we break through the fence that separates us from the higher levels, the serpentfire will burn away the dross of our lower desires that are like dust as it says: "...Dust is the serpents food.." (ISA. LXV, 25) It says further: "fiery serpents" They are so called because they burn the soul (Ḥukkath, 22) — and it is said further "...it was actually only one serpent..." (i.b. 23)

Terms:

— Vines=serpentfire

— Wine=Torah, Emanation of God

— Vineyards=Spiritual body, faith

— Fences=Gates of perception

All references in the Bible to the vines, to wine, clusters of grapes, vineyards and its fences, concern this part of the way, that is, "the time of the serpent."

> "...the fruit Eve did eat came from the spiraling vine...She took of the fruit thereof, and did eat. R. Aibu said: "She squeezed grapes and gave him..."
>
> Midrash Rabbah 19.5

Other phrases are: having more than one Vineyard — lusting for somebody else's vines — tilling or abandoning the yard — putting up a fence at the neighbor's yard — a vineyard of a person void of understanding — turned not by the way of the vineyards.

> "...And planted a vineyard. 'As He was going to plant the vineyard the spirit Shimadon (Shem-Adon=name of the Lord) met him and proposed: 'come into partnership with me, but take care not to enter into my portion, for if you do I will injure you' '...and he drank of the wine and was drunken (IX, 21)...R. Hiyya ben Ba said: "He planted it, drank thereof and was humiliated all on one and the same day.' 'Within his tent' he was uncovered in his wifes tent.' R. Huna said in R. Eliezer's name...'When Noah was leaving the ark a lion struck and mutilated him

(castrated). Now he went to cohabit, but his semen was scattered and he was humiliated..." R. Johannan commented upon Noah: "...Beware of a passion for wine, because in this passage on wine(Gen. IX) the word 'woe' is written 14 times..." ("woe" in hebrew=A.O.I.)

Midrash Rabbah 36:3-4 (Noah)

24. "...Thus the sun has never seen the black unshining face of the moon, no planet rises out of his turn before another; no planet beholds the one above it, for all planets revolve, so R. Levi said, as on a spiral staircase..."

Pesikta De-Rab. Kahana, P. 1

At the end of the purifications, when the severity of the "fire of Isaac" (the serpentfire) had burned the accumulated dross, (when the ram with the spiral horn is sacrificed), the old concepts of the self and life are destroyed. This is the sacrifical death of the hero, while still alive.

"...R. Hiya said: "This fire is the fire of Isaac, who said (at the time of the binding) "behold the fire and the wood (Gen 22: 7) which perpetually exists." We have learned that from the fire of Isaac there issues forth to the altar certain coals...Now there is on the altar a footway with a certain number of steps, and the lowest step reaches to the abyss which is the highest of six..."

Zohar. LAV, 4:30a

"The Angel with the flaming sword with a fire that turns this way or that way" is the guardian who stands before the gate that leads to the garden (Gate of the East). With the help of Gematria, the name of the sword (with the flames spiraling upwards) Ḥered is changed to Ḥarbod, the knife of circumcision. This has been explained before. The Rabbis said, "the flaming sword refers to the Torah..." hence "...and Adam knew his wife" (Midrash Rabbah Genesis 4.)

25. The understanding of the incident of the fiery serpents in the wilderness (Num. 21:6) depends upon the translation of the words Naḥashim-Ha-Seraphim whether they are the fiery serpents as it is commonly understood or serpent-angels. The serpent-angels so common religions have six wings and are called the Seraphim (plural in Hebrew), that hold serpents as staves in their hands and the accompanying emblems show them as being the powers in us.

"...Our sages have already stated — for him who has understanding — that all forces that reside in the body are angels..."

Maimonides: Guide

26. "...Set me as a seal upon thy heart, as a seal upon thine arm...

"The flashes thereof are flashes of fire, a very flame of the lord..."

Song of Songs 8:6

The Song of Songs is a lovesong to God:

"...The seal brings light and freedom from tribulations to Israel...and they heard a voice which was to free them from darkness...This is the angel of death, who is called darkness; so it says, "and the tables were the work of God" and the writing was the writing of God, graven upon the tables" (Ex. XXXII/16)

Midrash Rabbah Song of Songs 8:6:1-4

"...As a seal upon thine arm: This refers to the phylacteries..."

All this comes from the hand and since the heart is called "Beauty," the saying is applied here, "Thou shalt also be a crown of beauty in the hand of God." (ISA. LXII/3) "...but yet a crown may fall from the place so the proper words are given to us in ISA. LIX/16: "Behold, I have graven thee upon the palms of my hands..."

27. "...and I will bring you out from under the burden of the Egyptians" Ex. VI6) These are here four expressions of redemptions: "I will bring you out — I will deliver you — I will redeem you and I will take you..." The sages accordingly ordained 4 cups to be drunk on the eve of Passover or correspond with these four expressions, in order to fulfill the verse: I will lift up the cup of salvation, I call upon the name of the Lord.." (PS. CXVI, 13)

On this level of perfection, the work of Jacob, (not yet Israel) the fiery power of air is represented by the eagle.

> "...that spot is the central fire that surrounds the innermost fire. For there are three varieties of fire in that connection. The first is the fire that receives fire with joy, the two meeting each other in love and joy; the second is that of which it is written: 'and there was brightness to the fire' (EZEK 1, 13) it is the innermost fire which is joyful at the presence of the other fire. Then comes the third fire which surrounds that brightness and wherein resides the terror of severity for the punishment of the wicked..."
>
> Zohar. 4: 216A

The black is also the color of the third stage, as it says:

> "...when Moses was on the mount, the Holy One showed him the red fire, the green fire, the black fire, and the white fire and said to him: 'make the tabernacle in these colors for me, in the colors and not in the fire' (Ex 25, 40) after the pattern that is shown to thee on the mount."
>
> Midrash Rabbah EX 5:3

28. When the higher soul of the body is born, Nefesh, the physical soul departs. This is the story of Isaac returning from the sacrifice on the mount of *Moriah* (the root M/R is *Lord* and Iah is God, the cabalistic reading of the word Moriah is Lord God). He found his mother Sarah (Nefesh) death and at the same moment his future wife, Rebecah (higher soul) was born; she, the vehicle of the spirit is called in the next degree Rachel.

> "...and Isaac was 40 years old when he took Rebecah...The number 40 here, Rabbi Isaak said, has an esoteric significance, to wit, that Isaac when he took Rebecah comprised in himself the union of north and south and fire and water..."
>
> Zohar. 2:136b

The name of Rebecah's nurse is Deborah (bee), and she is "the sweet sound of the bee," heard when the actions of the soul are understood by the awareness. This sound of the bee, like all other signals, is not permanent, as it says:

> "...and Deborah the nurse of Rebecah died and was buried underneath the house of God and beneath an oak (the tree of life) and the name was called the oak that weepeth" (Alon-Bashut).

Historically, nobody was buried under or beside a house of worship at this time.
The Bible does not mention Rebecah's death since the emotions do not die. The root of the name Rebecah, R.B.C., is understood as:

— R=Dominion

— B=Life

— C=Palm of hand=Rebecah stands for dominion of life in the palm of the hand.

The root R.B.C. signifies further the higher soul in these words:

— *RECEB: Riding (in control of our animal nature)*

— *CHERUB*: Angel (powers of the self)

— ME*RCAB*AH: Charioth (ruaḥ, as the ascending vehicle of life)

All words that relate to the higher soul are in the Bible joined with the cypher four. Note this in the commenary to PS. LXUIII:4: "...him that rideth upon the Araboth (the highest heaven)..." do not read Araboth, but Arba-oth (the highest principles of the body (four)). With this in mind Philo translated araboth as the purified perfect mind. (See also Maimonides, Guide Chapt. 60)

The cipher four stands for the feast of the tabernacle (succoth) since it is held to commemorate the time that Israel had to live in the four walls (of his body), the booths on the way to the promised land.

"...I made the children of Israel to dwell in the booths when I brought them out of the land of Egypt..." (Lev. 23:43) Since the Israelites lived in tents and not in booths, it means that we hold "the feast of the Lord" (Lev. 23:39) to prepare the body as a habitation for the Lord. The rules concerning the feast and how to build a Tabernacle in the highest self are in the Torah and Talmud.

For seven days and seven nights we live, pray, eat, and sleep in inpermanent booths *made by our own hands.* Nobody can do that for us and most of the regulations concerning size, choice of building material, etc., have purely cabalistic significance. And adds T. Succah 41a. This: "...the great temple can be rebuild in one day...". To the seven days and seven nights, one day is added for each worshipper individually, so that the holidays last twice four days, to show that the subtle body is perfectly expanded. (Pesikta De-Rab Kahane, p. 28) To the ceremony of waterdrawing in the temple, Succah says:

> "...There are three golden candlesticks with four golden bowels on the top of each of them and four ladders...to each and four youths draw from priestly.."
>
> Talmud Succah 51a

The golden candlesticks with their seven arms and seven lights give the cypher fourteen. The four golden bowls, the four ladders and the four youths are the twelve tribes that surrounded the tabernacle during the sojourn in the wilderness.

The fiery serpents, called also the mythical beasts Leviathan and the Behemoth, (Pl.) are part of the feast.They rest near the water and are food for the righteous (both stand for the serpentfire). Not a hairsbreath distance is between those beasts and the skin of the Leviathan can be used rightfully to fill the cracks in the walls of the booth (Job 40:31).

"...on the place where the Leviathan rests," Said R. Kahana (S.2): "...is a shining of yellow gold, that means that the very place it lies upon is golden...The place where the Leviathan lies is purer even than yellow gold..." The commentaries that follow these statements show that the sage had been a cabalist.

The most remarkable traditions of "the feast" are related to the four minim (kinds of plants). Three species, the palm, myrtle, and the willows are elaborately fastened together (called Lulav), and held in the right hand during certain prayers and waved in all directions of the body. The fourth, a lemon-like fruit, the Ethrog, is held in the left hand like a king holding the globe. For the devout these fruits are the emblems for the powers of the body.

The plants relate to parts of the body: the Ethrog is the heart, the palm is the backbone, the myrtle, the eye (sing) and the willow is the organ of speech. The strips of the palm leaf that are woven spirally around those plants represent the bio-energies that hold the body together.

As the ancient sages saw it, the medicinal properties of these plants shed light on the regulations concerning purity. The willow helps against nocturnal emission and gives virility. The myrtle helps against high blood pressure, snakebite and brings general well-being. The ethrog cures uterine hemorrhages, while from the date-palm (backbone) everything can be used. Even its shadow was good, because Deborah (Bee) the prophetess judged here the people. This is obviously not a historical note.

The plants of the lulav are arranged in strict order with the myrtle on the left side (with at least two leaves, resembling so the sensing point of the spiritual eye). Our Rabbis taught, "...the plant that grows shaped as a plaid and resembles a chain is the myrtle." (Talmud Succah 32b). The palm is the center of the lulav as the backbone on the body. On the right side of the lulav is "the willow of the waters," a plant that had been placed before the Lord beside the many waters as it says, "that is Abraham and therefore the willow is on the right side of the lulav," and also, "under the willow rests the Behemoth..."

In the tradition, these four species of plants relate to the letters of the name of the Lord, *ADONOI*; the angels, Michael, Gabriel, Uriel and Raphael, the cultureheroes, Ephraim, Dan, Judah and Jacob; the elements, water, fire, air, and materia and the formative, learned, blessed and analytical levels of the self.

On each of the seven days of the festival one culturehero is invited to be a guest at the meal. This, again, is to tell us that we have to be like Abraham, Isaac, Jacob, Moses, Aaron, Joseph and David; in this order of succession.

29. After purification on the mount of Moriah, Isaac forty years old married Rebecah. On the side of pollution, his son Esau was also forty years old when he took the two wives Judith and Bashemot, "..which were a grief of mind unto Isaac and Rebecah..."

> "...You have deceived God at Sinai...you said, all that the Lord had spoken we will do and hear..."
>
> Midrash Rabbah Leviticus 7:4

And forty days later you said of the golden calf, "this is thy God o Israel..." (id, 32:4). Yet, "...the children of Israel ate mana forty years..." And, again on the side of pollution, "...and because they had murmered against the Lord...children shall wander in the wilderness for forty years..." though, "...these forty years the Lord thy God had been with thee, thou hast lacked nothing."

30. Pesikta D-Rab Kahane (concerning Joseph's brothers)

> "...You my brothers are part of the order of the universe, twelve hours in the day, twelve hours in the night, twelve months in a year, twelve signs in the Zodiac, twelve tribes of Israel..."
>
> P.16:5

This applies to Jacob and his twelve sons. His adversary, the twin brother Esau (negative force) is father of twelve nations that will fight "Israel" forever.

A few more examples: Levi and Joseph do not belong to the twelve tribes but the number is maintained by Israel adopting Joseph's children, Ephraim and Manasseh. "...and now thy two sons, Ephraim and Manasseh are mine: as Reu-ben and Simeon, they shall be mine." (Genesis 48:5).

Why are Reu-ben and Simeon mentioned with Ephraim and Manasseh?

The tribes are identified all through the scriptures and commentaries with the twelve functions of the body except that Reu-ben, (see my son) the sense of seeing, is superseded by Ephraim (fruitful) who stands for clairvoyancy. Likewise Simeon's (hearing) place is taken by Manasseh (turn of fortune), who is clairaudiency (Midrash Rabbah Numbers 14:21).

The ten other functions change during meditation. This is explained in Num. 10: "The names of the tribal patriarchs signify redemption and praise of the power of the Sheḥinah." Each one of them is an emissary of the subtle body and by this they become the guardians of gates to each side (level) of this body. The "sides of the body as the four levels has been mentioned before and the twelve on four levels are forty-eight, "gates to the palace."

There are two more gates in us, as was told before, one is the gate of the Shehinah and the other, the gate of Sod (secret), the cyphers forty-nine and fifty the sum of all the roads that can be passed in one lifetime. In their dual aspects as protectors and destroyers, the twelve are the "generations" of the Bible, mentioned twelve times (Midrash Rabbah 11:21). These are the "generations" that Adam had destroyed before his eye was opened. The twelve are also baskets with good fruit, the gates to heavenly Jerusalem, the legions of angels, sons, princes of Israel, houses, pillars, etc. Just like the fathers of the tribes, most of the twelve apostles of Christ are by no means well defined. Some are words of power like "the beloved disciple *IOA*NNIS (St. John) and others change their name. The Gnostics had twelve chief-priests that served "the enlightened". The Essenes termed them the twelve banners that lead the sons of the light in the war against the sons of darkness and called them tribes of the exile from the wilderness and sons of light. Twelve imams assisted Ali, the "lion of God" in Sufism; while the impersonator of the Mayan God Tezcatlipoca ruled for twelve months before his ceremonial slaying, his twelve constant companions guarded his body and gave him pleasure. The use of this number in the Mayan tradition is the more remarkable since the mayans used twenty months for the year and not twelve.

In the tales of King Arthur's round table (harboring tales from King David's court), twelve leading knights out of a number of seventy (cypher) conquered twelve kingdoms for him. In Upsala (sweden Up-Salam, (archaic) up-upper, Salam=peace), stood the great temple of God Don-Ar with twelve chairs for the deities of his realm. Likewise, did the Nordic Alfather Odin reign from his seat (Idavoll) in the center of the world (midgard=*guarding the center*) surrounded by twelve not very well defined rulers.

The signification of the twelve in the Bible: the tabernacle, our heart, protected on all sides by the twelve tribes and serviced by the Levites that do not own land or cattle but are on duty in all of Israel, resemble the functions of the spirit. The duties and regulations concerning the three (cypher) families of the tribe of Levi express the ideas concerning the functions of the blood that were current in ancient Israel.

The twelve that propel the six major sensing points are the twelve oxen that carry the Tabernacle is six covered wagons (Deut. 4:4), "how long are these oxen going to remain alive? As long as Israel cleaves to the Lord..." "...But ye that cleave unto the Lord your God are alive, everyone of you this day." (Midrash Rabbah Deut. 4:4).

The oxen were contributed by the twelve princes of Israel and whenever the tabernacle was erected in the wilderness it was guarded by the twelve tribes. In this, the tabernacle of the heart, God communicates with you.

The star of David as the symbol of the heart, has six points on the outside and six points that are formed by the powerstreams of the intertwined triangles. This emblem shows that you can control six of your bodily functions, while the others will follow once you have established mastery.

Beside the twelve stones on the breastplate of the high priest there are two mysterious powers hidden in the back of the shield called Urim and Thumim, *who advise and assist the high priest.* The word, 'Urim', from Or-the light means: that brings the fire (mih) of the inner light, i.e., clairvoyancy; and 'Thumim', "that his word is heard", clairaudiency.

Jacob had to serve for Leah seven years and another seven for Raḥel and on the third level he served six more years to inherit "the striped and speckled" trove. That was his work on the three levels and when he was perfected he had twelve sons. He and his sons are thirteen when he blesses them with six blessings.

> "...R. Simeon spoke: we have learnt" he said "that the knot of faith is tied with thirteen attributes and in addition the Torah is crowned with thirteen "measures" (rules of interpretation) and the holy Name is crowned therewith. Similarly when Jacob desired to bless his sons, he said that his sons should be blessed with the bonds of faith; it is written: "all these are the tribes of Israel, twelve and this (ZOTH) etc. (Genesis 49: 28). Thus there were thirteen, *the Shehinah being joined with them...'*
>
> Zohar. V. Ahare Moth 62a

The benefits that accrue from mastering the basic functions in the body are presented in a great variety of terms and tales: "human excellence is like the annointing oil: '"12 logs of oil was sufficient for the forty years of wandering in the wilderness." (Midrash Rabbah 33:3). Why did God remember Noah in his favor? Because being in the ark for twelve months, he provided for the animals (only) for the sake of pure sacrifices.

The significance of the tribes guarding the tabernacle and the order of their advance during the forty years is worth a detailed study. The first place on the east side (the place of the foundation) is reserved for the work of the Torah. The tribe of Juda (word) is the leader as the creative word of power, represented on the highest level as Angel Gabriel (Gibor-El=Mighty in God).

The tribes of Zebulun (sex-drive, bio-energy) and Issahar (work), the custodian of the Torah, are the assistents of Judah.

Judah, as the leader, is the King of all the life forces. Cabalistically his name means, "the door to God." How do we derive at such reading? Judah is written in Hebrew IHVDH, the letter D stands for *d*oor=*d*eleth, the other letters are the name of God, IHVH. It is said in M.R. Naso XIII, 4, "...By Judah God is known..."

In the first place on the southside is Reuben (sight). As the right hand he brings to the awareness all precepts of the Torah that had not been observed. The angel Mihael (mi-Ha-El=Who is like the Lord) is the name of the power and the help for right observation of the Torah come from Simeon (hearing) and Gad movement.

The westside of the tabernacle (head) guards and protects the heart and gives the strength of conviction to the work. The angel Raphael (rofe-El=God the healer) guides Ephraim (clairvoyancy), Manasseh (clairaudiency) and Benjamin (sleep).

We should note that Benjamin did not at first go down to Egypt with his brothers since in Egypt, the physical life, only one part of the sleep is for rest. The other parts of the sleep are used by the initiates to advance to the source of all.

Camped on the northside and protecting the rear of all the tribes are the tribes of the left hand. The angel Uriel (light of God) dispenses the fire of the Torah, even though the three tribes are apt to delay the work. Dan (thought) interferes with the holy precepts. Asher brings happiness to the work and Naphtali (food) is rather bothersome since he has to receive each day his share of the Mana in the wilderness.

The tribes come from *four* mothers and Rab. Kahana adds to this, "...Joseph said further: "before you (the tribes) came down to Egypt, the Egyptians treated me like a slave. But once you came down here to Egypt, you made known my honorable lineage..." This statement is worth considering.

31. These powers are the, "Aserah Sefirot Beli-Mah" translated "the ten ineffable spheres" Beli-Mah ('Zahlen ohne alles" or 'intangible Sefirot"). For cabalists this phrase means: ten forcefieds, active in and beyond the universe (beyond the world, time, or space).

> "...ten Sephirot Beli-mah, like the numbers of fingers, five that are *against* five and one covenant between them: the circumcision of the word and circumcision of the flesh..."
>
> Book of Formation 1:3

I had explained before how the work of the left hand (fire) stands in opposition to the right hand (water) and because of this incompatibility of our forces, we progress. These are the five that are *against* the five, just as the animals our dark forces were created. "...I will make him a help that is *against* him..." (Gen. 2:18). These are the beasts that have to be sacrificed in the heart (tabernacle) and are further explained:

> "...thou shall couple the curtains" "The curtains of the Tabernacle were coupled in two groups, each having five curtains..." "and it shall be one." Moses coupled those curtains each of the seven days..." (Cypher seventy)
>
> Midrash Rabbah Ex. 26:6

32. These forces that seem to stream in spirals are euphemistically compared to *animals*; to the hinds, gazelles or goats going up or down the mountain (spiritual body) or in the wilderness

> "...at the time that the flock conceived, ...I (Jacob) lifted up mine eye (sing) and saw in a dream, and behold the he-goats streaked, speckled or grizzled..."
>
> Genesis 31:10

> "...we have already explained at great length that in the beginning the emanations of the *MOST HIGH* are streaked, speckled and spotted..." "...the light extended further downwards from the afore mentioned aspect known as streaked and then became ten vessels..."
>
> "Tree of Life" Haim Vital

The wood that Jacob had put into the *watering* troughs was from the tree of life, and made the animals "ringstreaked, speckled and spotted." The veils, curtains, clouds have identical meaning.

> "...Ten sephirot beli-mah: they are like lightening, their goal infinite. HIS *word* is in them when they emanate or return. They haste like the storm and prostrate before his throne..."
>
> Book of Formation 1:6

33. These three levels are represented by the three mysterious ascends of Moses (Ex.

LIST NUMBER FOUR

THE TWENTY-TWO BUILDINGSTONES OF THE UNIVERSE AND MAN

LETTER	NUMBER	NAME		SIGNIFICATION	ASTRO	ON THE BODY	IN THE UNIVERSE	IN TIME	RULE	IN THE OCCULT WORK
א	1	ALEF	A	OX	🜁		AIR ATMOSPHERE	SPRING AUTUMN		MERIT
ב	2	BET	B	HOUSE	☉	RIGHT EYE	ABOVE SUN	SUNDAY	MYSTERY OF THE RULE OF GRACE	WISDOM FOLLY
ג	3	GIMMEL	G	CAMEL	☽	LEFT EYE	BELOW MOON	MONDAY		PEACE WAR
ד	4	DALET	D	DOOR	♎	RIGHT EAR	EAST LIBRA	TUESDAY		BEAUTY UGLINESS
ה	5	HAY	H	WINDOW	♍	RIGHT HAND	VIRGO	ELUL MARCH		SIGHT
ו	6	VAV	O	PEG NAIL	♉	LEFT HAND	TAURUS	IJAR APRIL		HEARING
ז	7	ZAJIN	Z	SWORD	♊	RIGHT FOOT	GEMINI	SIVAN MAY		SMELL
ח	8	HET	H	FENCE ENCLOSURE	♏	LEFT FOOT	SCORPIO	HASVAN JUNE		SPEECH
ט	9	TET	T	SERPENT	♌	RIGHT KIDNEY	LEO	AB JULY	MYSTERY OF THE RULE OF MERCY	TASTE
י	10	YOD	I	HAND	♈	LEFT KIDNEY	ARIES	NISAN AUGUST		COITION
כ	20	KAV	K	PALM OF HAND	♃	LEFT EAR	WEST JUPITER	WEDNESDAY		HEALTH POVERTY
ל	30	LAMET	L	OX GOAD	♂	LIVER	MARS	TISHRI SEPTEMBER		WORK
מ	40	MEM	M	WATER		BELLY	WATER EARTH	WINTER COLD		GUILT
נ	50	NOON	N	FISH	♋	SPLEEN	CANCER	TAMUZ OCTOBER		MOVEMENT
ס	60	SAMEH	S	PROP SUPPORT	♐	GALL	SAGITARIUS	KISLEV NOVEMBER		WRATH
ע	70	I-IN	E	EYE	♑	STOMACH	CAPRICORN	TEVET DECEMBER	MYSTERY OF THE STRICT RULE OF JUSTICE	MIRTH
פ	80	PEH	P	MOUTH	♀	RIGHT NOSTRIL	NORTH VENUS	THURSDAY		LIFE DEATH
צ	90	ZADEK	TZ	FISH HOOK	♒	COLON	AQUARIUS	SEVATH JANUARY		MEDITATION
ק	100	KAFF	Q	BACK OF HEAD	♓	BOWELS	PISCES	ADAR FEBRUARY		SLEEP
ר	200	RESH	R	HEAD	☿	LEFT NOSTRIL	SOUTH MERCURY	FRIDAY		FRUITFULL STERIL
ש	300	SHIN	SH	TEETH		HEAD	HEAVEN	SUMMER HEAT		LAW
ת	400	TAFF	TH	SIGN ON FOREHEAD	♄	MOUTH	CENTER SATURN	SATURDAY		DOMINON SLAVERY

The twentytwo letters of the Hebrew alphabeth reveal through their forms, sounds and position in a word the nature and actions of supernal powers. When the letters are understood in their cabalistic sense, they become tools of the initiate and the words change into forces that form, maintain and improve life. Hidden paths are revealed when words are formed or existing ones changed by adding, removing or by the transfer of letters.

ACTING LEVELS	POWER WORDS	CABALISTIC ASPECTS	ASPECTS OF TAROT		
			TAROT	GEMS METALS	ASTRO
MICROCOSMIC OR ATOMIC LEVEL.	ELOHIM	UNITY, INFINITE, 1000	FOOL JOGLER	QUICK-SILVER	MERCURY
		BETH (HOUSE) BENEDICTION, BERAHOT, BUSINESS, DUALITY	EMPEROR	SILVER	VIRGO
		GIVING, GEMUL, GENES, UNDERSTANDING	EMPRESS	IRON	LIBRA
		OPENING, RECEIVING, CHANNEL, DRY LAND	FEMALE POPE	COPPER	SCORPIO
		SOUL, HUMANITY, LOVE, INITIATION	POPE		JUPITER
		PHALLUS, PROCREATIVE LIFEFORCES TRUTH, HEAVEN, UNITY, BINDING	LOVERS		VENUS
		VIBRATING SPIRITUAL FORCES, REMEMBRANCE, SICARON	CHARIOTH	CARBUNCLE	SAGITARIUS
		EMOTIONS, SYNTHESIS, SIN	JUSTICE	ONYX	CAPRICORN
		GOOD, TOV, LAW	HERMIT	SAPHIRE	AQUARIUS
CENTRAL AGENT		. CHANNEL OF GODS WILL, CHANGE OF FORTUNE LAW OF TRANSFORMATION	WHEEL OF FORTUNE	RADIUM	URANUS
IONIC LEVEL	ADONOI	HONOR, KAVOTH, CURSE, QUANTITY, EXTERMINATION, KELAYIAH	STRENGHT	TIN	NEPTUNE
		CENTER OF ALL, TEACHER, LIMUD, LEADER, LERNEN POSSESSION.	HANGED MAN	PERIDOT	PISCES
		MULTIPLICATION, MOTHER, MASSES, ILLUSION, MAG: MAHATMA	DEATH	AMETHYST	ARIES
		COMELY, FALLEN, NUCLEUS, NAVA, NEFILLIM, EGO, CAN NOT BE JOINED	TEMPERANCE	AGATE	TAURUS
		~~TOUPHOLD~~, BOUNDARY OF MATTER, SEMIHA, MANIFESTATION TRESHOLD, SATAN, SHET.	DEVIL	LEAD	SATURN
		HUMILITY, INQUITY, SOURCE, ANAVA AWON SPRING	TOWER		MARS
		REDEMPTION, TRANSGRESSION, PURHANA, PESHA	STAR	BERYL	GEMINI
		RIGHTEOUS, LAW OF THE MACROCOSM, ZADDIK, ORGANISER, HIDDEN	MOON	EMERALD	CANCER
MACROCOSMIC LEVEL	IHVH	PENETRATION, MULTIPLICATION, DIGGING	SUN	RUBY	LEO
		MOVEMENT, FIRM, CLEAN, VIBRATION, EVIL=RA, RESURRECTION, ROY, KING, MASTER, DOMINION (RIDING)	MAGICIAN	MERCURY	MOON
		SHINY RADIATION, SHADDAY, TRUTH, WISDON, SUPERNAL FIRE, COAT OF LIGHT	MAGUS		SUN
		ULTIMATE CONDITION, DISSOLVE, ABOLISH	WORLD	GOLD	EARTH

19:3), "...and Moses went up to God of the Elohim..." where he was offered the covenant and the people said, "...all that IHVH had said we will do..." (Exodus 19:8). On the second ascend the Lord came in a *thick cloud*; the commandments were given and again they said ..."all the words IHVH hath said we will do"... (Ex. 24:5). However when the words were read to Israel they sacrificed the animal (nature) and answered, "...we do and will hear"...(Ex. 24:7). They were sprinkled with the blood of the sacrifices and could hear God because they had accepted the Law.

LIST NUMBER TWO

The Twelve Simples

	NAME AND TRANSLATION	LETTER	FUNCTION	SIGNIFY		ESCUCHEON	COLOR	BODY	GUARD THE ALTAR	MOTHERS	ASTRO	YEAR	UNIVERS	STONES	CHRISTIAN APOSTLES	HINDU MAHA-NARAYANA
1	REUBEN SEE MY SON	YOT	SIGHT	PENITENCE	REPENTANCE FOR NOT HAVING OBSERVED THE PRECEPT OF TORAH	MANDRAKE	WHITE	RIGHT HAND	SOUTH		♈	3/21-4/19 NISAN	ARIES	RUBY	JUDE	SATYAN TRUTH
2	SIMEON HEAR	V VAV	HEARING	ATONEMENT	VIOLENCE	TOWN OF SHEHEM	GREEN LION	LIVER	SOUTH		♉	4/20-5/20 IYAR	TAURUS	TOPAZ	SIMON	TAPAS FASTING
3	LEVY REGARD	SS ZAJIN	SMELL	TABERNACLE	ESCORT TO GOD,, HEART LEVAYAH, LEADER	URIM & THUMIM	RED, WHITE BLACK	RIGHT FOOT	CENTER		♊	5/21-6/22 SIVAN	SUN GEMINI	SMARAGD	MATHEWS	DAMA SUBDUING
4	JUDAH PRAISE	N NUN	SPEECH WORD	RULER	GOOD SENSE,PRAISE,LEARNING,WISDOM	LION AARON'S SONS	RED LION	LEFT FOOT	EAST		♋	6/23-7/22 TAMUZ	MOON CANCER	CARBUNCLE	MARK	CAMA TRANQUILITY
5	ISSAHAR MAN OF REWARD	T TET	WORK OF THE TORAH	SCRIBE	CUSTODIAN OF THE TORAH,ASTROLOGER NOBLE DEEDS, SCHOLAR	SUN & MOON	BLACK	RIGHT KIDNEY	EAST	LEAH	♌	7/23-8/22 AB	LEO	SAPHIRE	JAMES THE GREATER	DANAM CHARITY
6	ZEBULUN KEEN	H HEH	COITION	WEALTH		SHIP	SILVER WHITE	LEFT KIDNEY	EAST		♍	8/23-9/24 ELUL	VIRGO	EMERALD	PETER	DHARMA DUTY
7	DAN JUDGE	D DALETH	THOUGHT	DARKNESS	ANALYTIC MIND, JUDGE,FLYING SERPENT DISTINGUISHED	TWO-HORNED SERPENT	BLACK	LEFT HAND	NORTH		♎	9/25-10/23 TISHRI	LIBRA	JACINTH	JAMES THE LESS	PRAJANA PROCREATION
8	NAFTALI CONTEST	H CHET	FOOD	SATISFACTION	PEACE	HIND	RED	MILT	NORTH	BILHA	♏	10/24-11/22 HESHVAN	scorpio	beryl	luke	agnayam FIRE
9	GAD FORTUNE	S SAMEH	PASSION	STRENGHT	RECEIVING SUSTENANCE,,SUFFICIENCY	CAMP	GRAY	GALL	SOUTH		♐	11/23-12/21 KISLEV	SAGITARIUS	AGATE	ANDREW	AGNI HOTRAM WATER
10	ASHER FORTUNE	O I-IN	PLEASURE	LIGHT	VISIBLE,WEALTH,ASHERA	OLIVE TREE		STOMACH	NORTH	ZILPA	♑	12/22-1/2 TEVETH	CAPRICORN	AMETYST	BARTHOLOMEW	JAYNA SACRIFICES
11	JOSEF END. IN GOD	Z TSADE	MEDITATION	PERFECTION		MAP OF EGYPT	ALL COLORS	RENNET BAG			♒	1/21-2/19 SEVATH	AQUARIUS	ONYX	JUDAS ISCHARIOTH	MANASAM SPIRITUALISM
12	BEN-JAMIN SON OF THE RIGHT	OU CAF	SLEEP	POWER	VAINGLORY	WOLF	BLACK	BOWLS	WEST	RAHEL	♓	2/20-3/20 ADAR	PISCES	JASPER	JOHN	NAYSA RENUNCIATION
1	EFRAIM FRUITFFULL			CLAIRVOYANCE	URIM	OX	BLUE		WEST							
2	MANASSEH LUCK			CLAIRAUDIENT	THUMIM	WILD BULL	DEEP BLACK		WEST	ASENATH						

Of the twelve constant functions of the human body, only six can be controlled. The others will only gradually relinquish their hold. How these functions act on the physical, emotional, intellectual and spiritual levels is told in the story of the four mothers of the tribes. The mothers are the perceptions that form, influence and guide the actions. The name of Leah (written L.A.H.) is understood as "the benefits of diligence"; she perceived only physical matters and hence: "her eyes were weak". Her sons were: sight, hearing, smell, speech, diligences in the work of the Torah and sex drive. The name of Leah's handmaid Zilpah (SS.L.P.) means "creating fragrance in life" These are the emotions and her sons were passion and pleasure. And do not our passions and pleasures bring fragrance to life? The handmaid of Rahel is Bilha (B.L.H.), cabalistically translated as the "understanding of creation" on the intellectual level. Her offsprings are Dan, the thought and Naftali (contest) the disputation. The name Rahel is explained as Ruaḥ-El, however the cabalists read it as:

R=the change from sterile to fertile

H=the word of God

L=the work of perfection, so that the word Rahel means "the word of God changes sterility to abundance" during the work of perfection. This is done on the spiritual level.

Now, Rahel had been sterile for a long time before giving birth to Josef who is prayer and meditation and Benjamin, the son of the right hand (or way), who is emblematic for the "sleep of the magician".

The four mothers, levels, sides of the temple, directions of the tabernacle and the microcosm, are also south or right hand, the north, that is the left hand, east the foundation and the head in the west.

LIST NUMBER ONE

The Seven Doubles

SENSE ORGANS	SYMBOLS: LETTER	SYMBOLS: ASTRO	SYMBOLS: MAGIC	SYMBOLS: HINDU	LOCATION ON THE BODY AND REVELATION	PERMUTATION & FOUNDATION		METAL	REMARKS	TERMS FOR CIPHER SEVEN IN HINDUISM: CHACRA NAME	GUARDIAN	MANDALA	HINDU ASPECTS
KETHER Crown, Supernal Knowledge	ת	♄ SATURN	♒ ♑	△	CROWN OF HEAD GOD	FROM AVARICE, SLAVERY TO POWER, DOMINION	CENTER OF HOLY TEMPLE, SABBATH	GOLD	ALL LETTERS OF THE ALPHABET ARE IN THIS POINT	SAHASRARA	YAKSHIN SHANKINI	CHANDRA	STHULABHUTA
HAHMA Wisdom	ב	☉ SUN	♍ ♄ ♌	▽	EYE APPEARANCE	KNOWLEDGE, FOLLY TO WISDOM, FEAR OF GOD	ABOVE SUNDAY	SILVER		AJNA	HAKINI BODINI	NABHO	BUDDHI:
BINAH Understanding	ג	☽ MOON	♋	○	THROAT VISION	ANGER, MISFORTUNE TO PEACE, MEEKNESS	BELOW MONDAY	IRON		VISHUDDHA	SHAKINI	VAYU	KAMA BODY
HESED Supernal Love	ד	♎ LIBRA	♈ ♏ ♎	✡	HEART REVELATION	UGLINESS TO PASSION, BEAUTY AND LOVE OF GOD	NORTH TUESDAY	COPPER	SOURCE OF PROSPERITY	ANAHATA	KAKINI	VAHNI	ATMA
RAHAMIM Pity	כ	♃ JUPITER	♐ ♓	[illegible]	NAVEL ASPECTS	POVERTY, GREED TO WEALTH, GENEROSITY	WEST WEDNESDAY	TIN	ILLUSIONS CREATED OR DESTROYED	MANIPURA	LAKINI	JALA	ETHER PRANA
PAHAD Fear	פ	♀ VENUS	♉	□	SEX ORGAN WORD	DEATH TO DIVINE LOVE	EAST THURSDAY	LEAD		SVADISHTHANA	RAKINI	BHU	KAMAMANAS
NEZAH Firmness	ר	☿ MERCURY	♍ ♊	[illegible]	FOUNDATION BURDEN	STERILITY, HUNGER TO SPIRITUAL CONTENT	SOUTH FRIDAY	MERCURY	SOUND OF BEES; PLACE OF THE LION; UNIT OF THE ELEMENTS	MULADHARA	DAHINI		BUDDHIMANAS

LIST NUMBER THREE

THE TEN FORCEFIELDS

TEN FORCEFIELDS	ALTERNATE NAMES	ON THE BODY	WORD OF POWER	LOCATION ON THE TREE	COLOR	ZOHARIC HEROES	ANGELS	REMARKS	HINDUISM			CHRISTIANITY	
									CARDINAL VIRTUES	PANTHEON	DIRECTIONS	BODY OF CHRIST	EMBLEMS
KETHER CROWN KNOWLEDGE	DAAT FAITH	CROWN OF HEAD	YEHIEH	MIDDLE PILLAR FORMATION	GREEN	MESSIAH	METATRON		KNOWLEDGE	BRAHMA	ABOVE	CROWN OF THORNS	CROWN
HOHMA WISDOM	FATHER	FOREHEAD	ADONOI IHVH	RIGHT PILLAR FORMATION	WHITE	SOLOMON	RAZIEL	ARCHITECT OF THE CREATION	WISDOM PRAJÑA	INDRA	EAST	FOREHEAD	HAND WITH TRIANGLE
BINAH UNDERSTANDING	MYSTERY OF WINE	TROATH	ADONOI ELOHENU	LEFT PILLAR FORMATION	WHITE	DAVID	TSAFKIEL	THE WORLD OF TRANSCENDENTAL FREEDOM	PRAYER PRANIDANA	YAMA	BELOW	RIGHT PALM	EYE
TIFERET BEAUTY	LEV HASHAMAYIM HEART OF HEAVEN	HEART	ADONOI EL	MIDDLE PILLAR EMOTIONS	GREEN	ABRAHAM	TSADKIEL	SUN LIFE OF THE WORLD	CHARITY DANA	VARUNA WATER	SOUTHEAST	LEFT PALM	FIGHTER
DIN JUDGEMENT	GEVURAH PAHAD STRENGHT	MILT	ADONOI EL GIBBOR	LEFT PILLAR EMOTION	RED	ISAAC	SAMAEL	DUST ISAAC	METHOD UPAYA	AGNI FIRE	NORTHWEST	HEART	PRAYING MAN
RAHAMIM MERCY	HESED KINDNESS LOVE	LIVER	ADONOI IHVH	RIGHT PILLAR EMOTIONS	GREEN	ISRAEL JACOB	RAFAEL	ARTIFICER OF FORMATION	INDUSTRY VIRYA	VAYU AIR	SOUTHWEST	WOUND ON THE LOIN	SUN
NEZAH FIRMNESS	PERPETUITY ETERNITY	KNEE	IHVH ZABAOT	RIGHT PILLAR PHYSICAL	WHITE	MOSES	KANIEL		FORTITUDE BALA	SURA	SOUTH	RIGHT FOOT	MAN CARRIES UNIVERSE
HOD MAJESTY	SPLENDOR HONOR GLORY	KNEE	ADONOI SHADAY	LEFT PILLAR PHYSICAL	RED	AARON	MIHAEL		MORALITY SILA	BHUPATI	NORTH	LEFT FOOT	CANDLE STICK
JESOD HA-OLAM FOUNDATION	ZADDIK GATHERING OF THE WATER	ORGAN	ADONOI	MIDDLE PILLAR PHYSICAL	GREEN	MIRIAM	GABRIEL	BOOK OF REMEMBRANCE	PATIENCE SHANTI	YAKSHAS	WEST	LOIN CLOTH	CHALICE
MALKUTH KINGSHIP	HOLY CITY DELIVER	FEET	ADONOI MELEH	ROOT PHYSICAL TREE OF DEATH	GREEN	SHEHINAH	SANDAL-FON	YEAR OF REMISSION MOON	MEDITATION DHYANA	SOMA	NORTHEAST		CHALICE WITH SERPENT

LIST NUMBER ONE

The Seven Doubles

WORDS OF POWER					BENEFITS & GRADES OF THE ORGANS (E.S.P.)	# OF PETALS	ASPECTS OF THE			COLORS
HEAVENS	MAGIC	ANGELS GUARDIANS	HINDU	SUFI			CULTURE-HEROES	TEACHERS	WORLDS	
ARABOTH ARATRON		CASSI-EL	HAMSA A	ALLAH	HIGHEST EMANATION KNOWLEDGE OF MAGIC	1000	MOSES	ENOSH	TEBEL	BRILLIANCE
MAON MA EHEN MAH ZEN		MI-HA-EL	MA OM	HOU	CLAIRVOYANCE GRADE OF THE SAGE	2	AMRAM	JARED	NESHIYYAH	WHITE
ZEBUL		GABRI-EL	HAM	A.L.M ALOHIM	CLAIRAUDIENCE CENTER OF LIFEFORCES HEALING	8 16	KOHATH	MAHALALEL	ZIYYA	PURPLE
SHEHAKIM PHALES MAHON HAZON		SA-MA-EL	YAM	A.L.M.R.	INFLUENCE POWER OF ADVANCEMENT TOUCH	6 12 18 24	LEVY	KENAN	GE	YELLOW
RAKIAH BETHOR ZEBUL HAZOTH		SA-HI-EL	MAM VAM	TA-HA	MAGIC POWER SPIRITUAL HAND FEELINGS GRADE OF DIGNITY	10	JACOB	ENOSH	ARHA	BLUE
SHEMEI HASHAMAYIM HAGITH SAGUN		ANA-EL	LAM KA	YASIN	GENERATIVE FORCES GRADE OF HARMONY BALANCE	6	ISAAC	SETH	ADAMAH	VERMILLION OFF WHITE
SHAMAYIM OPHIEL RAQUIA HEZYON		OPHI-EL	KAMA	RA	SMELL GRADE OF MAGICAL ARTS	4	ABRAHAM	ADAM	EREL	GOLD